A SAILING
Malaysia
Mediterranean

Lloyd Price

© 2013 Malcolm Lloyd Price
All rights reserved.

ISBN: 1492151262
ISBN-13: 9781492151265

Library of Congress Control Number: 2012916439
CreateSpace Independent Publishing Platform
North Charleston, South Carolina

Route taken from Malaysia to Mediterranean ...
January through June 2010

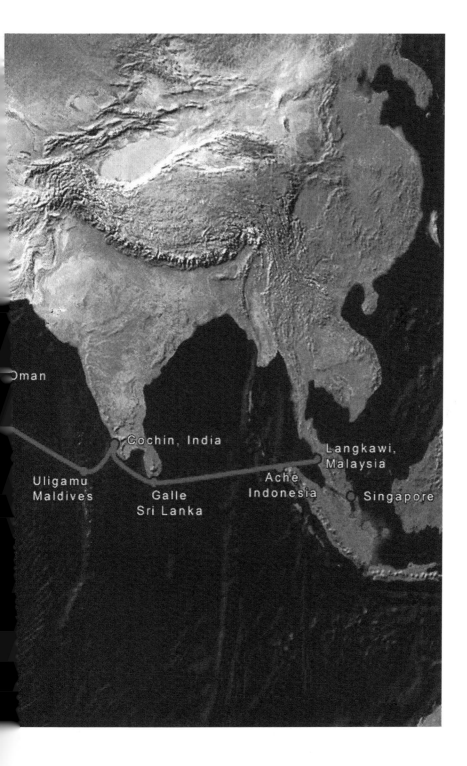

ACKNOWLEDGEMENTS:

Firstly, I want to thank Bebe Speed alias 'Bravo'... *(Why Bravo? Well Bebe is pronounced 'BB' and readily equates to 'Bravo Bravo' from the phonetic alphabet and I then shortened it to Bravo. Simple aye?)* for the tremendous number of hours she put into editing this book. Bravo was never backward in suggesting a correction to anything I'd written about the **Malaysia to Mediterranean** journey that she didn't quite understand. I'm sure she has read the text so many times she must now feel she was with me on Déjà vu III throughout the journey. Valuable though her editing was, I did baulk at considering her suggestion to use the word 'doddle' rather than 'piece-of-cake' at a particular point in the text! Her proposition made me realise the *big* gap there is sometimes between English and Australian languages and of course I chose to stick with the Auzzie version.

Bravo has sailed with me four times up to 2012; Borneo (2009), Greece (2010) and Croatia (2011) and Malta (2012).

Graham Upton, Bebe's husband, a twice retired Vice Chancellor in the UK (firstly in 2007 from Oxford Brookes University and secondly from University of Cumbria) gave me valuable advice on book titles, internet publishing and many other aspects of writing a book. He made it seem so easy! A very intelligent man willing to offer advice to a novice writer which was greatly appreciated.

DEDICATION:

I dedicate this book to my daughters Melanie and Arianne and my pesky granddaughter *(GD)* Sienna.

I leant hard on Melanie at times when I wanted an opinion on something technical *(she's a clever girl and voluminous reader)* and she always gave advice which I benefited from.

My other clever, artistic daughter Arianne always kept in touch, supplying essential goods not available in the region I was sailing and constantly checking to make sure her Dad was healthy and had not yet ***drifted to the Antarctic!***

And **GD** ... well, at four-and-a-half years old, she is an explosive bundle of energy and quite loveable as only granddaughters can be ... but, the one great regret I have of my cruising lifestyle is that I am missing her growing up ... ***and yes, she is 'pesky'!***

I Love them all!

CONTENTS

ACKNOWLEDGEMENTS: vii
DEDICATION: ix
CONTENTS xi
PREFACE xiii
Chapter 1 PREPARATIONS FOR M2M JOURNEY 1
Chapter 2 LANGKAWI, MALAYSIA TO ACEH, INDONESIA 27
Chapter 3 ACEH, INDONESIA TO GALLE, SRI LANKA 35
Chapter 4 GALLE, SRI LANKA TO COCHIN, INDIA. 47
Chapter 5 COCHIN, INDIA TO THE MALDIVE ISLANDS. 57
Chapter 6 THE MALDIVE ISLANDS to SALALAH, OMAN. 65
Chapter 7 SALALAH, OMAN 77
Chapter 8 SALALAH, OMAN to AL MUKALLA, YEMEN 87
Chapter 9 AL MUKALLA to ADEN, YEMEN 97
Chapter 10 ADEN, YEMEN 103
Chapter 11 ADEN, YEMEN TO PORT MASSAWA, ERITREA 115
Chapter 12 PORT MASSAWA, ERITREA. 125
Chapter 13 PORT SUWAKIN, SUDAN 135
Chapter 14 PORT LULI, EGYPT. 149
Chapter 15 PORT GHALIB, EGYPT 155
Chapter 16 HURGHADA, TO PORT SUEZ, EGYPT 165
Chapter 17 SUEZ CANAL PASSAGE 179
Chapter 18 PAPHOS, CYPRUS. 185
Chapter 19 FINEKE, TURKEY. 191

PREFACE

This is a story about how a fairly ordinary guy knowing almost nothing about blue water sailing and having never strayed further than 20 miles from his yacht club, ended up sailing a 10 metre catamaran yacht from *Australia to the Mediterranean.*

My working life, latterly as a local government administration officer for the Town of Cambridge in Western Australia, had ended in August 2004 when I retired at the age of 65. My marriage of 40 years ended in an amicable separation at roughly the same time, after which I decided to change my lifestyle dramatically and rather than buying a house, bought a four-year-old 10 metre (33ft) Seawind 1000 catamaran yacht.

Another factor in such a radical life-change had been reading the website of Seawind Catamarans and noticing a web page written by Joe Ziudzinski about the story of his and his wife Kathy's adventures on their Seawind 1000, 'Katie Kat'. Be warned, should you go to the website you may just find yourself buying a Seawind Catamaran as well!

I have to confess I was a completely novice bluewater sailor when I made that purchase in Sydney, New South Wales, Australia. My only sailing experience had been sailing and racing 14' beach catamarans for a few years and I assumed that having had the experience of tacking a 14'er it shouldn't be much harder to tack a 33' catamaran and my thinking was close to the truth.

So it was, in October 2004, having gathered almost all my worldly possessions and stored them with loving daughters Melanie and Arianne, I packed my wagon and drove across Australia to my new floating home in Sydney ... then named 'SV Tsunami' (later to be renamed 'Déjà vu III'). On boarding 'Tsunami' late in October 2004, I set myself a learning programme for the next three months and ended up exploring many of the beautiful bays of Pittwater and the Hawkesbury River, 15 nautical miles (nmiles) north of Sydney, New South Wales, Australia. Initially, this was all by motor power which was relatively easy as I had owned a 23ft powerboat for three years.

The time had to come, however, when I had to venture into the world of sailing ... so I cautiously raised the sails, one at a time, starting with the smallest jib. In hindsight I'm not sure Pittwater was the best place to learn as the winds swirl madly around these waters making 'simple' sailing (by 'simple' I mean sailing for 10 nmiles without changing a sail setting) a significant challenge. But maybe this was the best way to learn ... *fast?*

After 6 or 7 weeks I made the momentous decision to enter the Tasman Sea and sail to Sydney Harbour. **Wow, this was a giant step** ... after all 'The Harbour' is a vast distance of 15 nmiles south over open sea and I felt as Captain Cook must have felt sailing to the edge-of-the-world ... *very nervous!*

But I managed it, though an even greater learning experience was sailing around the harbour itself. Any novice who sails around Sydney Harbour for six weeks without hitting another vessel, rock, pier, wharf, pontoon or Manley Ferry will have succeeded in passing a significant lesson in a deep-blue-water apprenticeship!

In the subsequent two and a half years, I sailed, mostly solo, many nmiles up and down the east coast of Australia branching out north to Lizard Island, Queensland, twice, then south to Tasmania and east to Lord Howe Island, always learning as I went. By then, I had seen most anchorages along the east coast of Australia up to six times and I was getting bored, so I joined a Rally out of Darwin, in the Northern Territory of Australia, which had lured around 100 other yachts from all around the world. We left Darwin mid July, 2007 and the schedule took us through Indonesia and on to Singapore on a four month journey.

From Singapore I ventured up the west coastline of Malaysia and migrated, along with many of my new rally friends, to the Rebak Marina on a small island out from Langkawi. From here we went our own ways and I sailed north to Thailand and then shuttled between the two countries for about 19 months.

It was time for a change again and I joined a second rally which was taking a small fleet from Penang Island *(west coast of Malaysia)* down to Singapore and up the east coast of Malaysia to Terengganu. From there we sailed across the South China Sea to Kuching, Borneo and then north along the west coast

A SAILING ODYSSEY-Malaysia to the Mediterranean

Upper - Approaching Puteri Harbour Marina-new Government building on hill ahead
Lower - Safely berthed at Puteri Harbour Marina, Malaysia.

> *Hard to explain then why, at the age of 73, I find myself living onboard a 10 metre catamaran in Italy ... maybe its contentment?*

of Borneo, calling into Brunei and onto the Malaysian city of Kota Kinabalu in Sabah.

With all this experience behind me, I felt ready to tackle the *Malaysia to Mediterranean journey (M2M)*. At that point I had been sailing DJV for over five years and had experienced many exciting moments, but it's the *M2M* that I have chosen for the focus of this, my first book. Most people I speak to are particularly interested in this leg of what, for me, may eventually turn into a circumnavigation of our great planet: maybe it's the threat of piracy, or the mystique of Indian and Arabian countries which draws them to this part of my journey.

As of August 2012 and with the *M2M* now far behind me, I've sailed DJV, mostly solo, 34,000 nmiles and although I've inadvertently done some horrible things to the little Seawind 1000, we're still friends and I still love her! I see myself as a much more experienced man of the sea now, surprising myself more than anyone given I was born to a farming couple, in the rural area of Cunderdin, 160 kilometres east of the state capital Perth in Western Australia. I was introduced to open ocean swimming at the age of 15 and never developed a liking for it and am still a poor swimmer. I never harboured any dream of 'sailing-over-the-horizon'. Hard to explain then why, at the age of 73, I find myself living on-board a 10 metre catamaran in Italy having sailed here from Australia through Indonesia, Singapore, Malaysia, Thailand, Borneo, Sri Lanka, India, The Maldives, Oman, Yemen, Eritrea, Sudan, Egypt, Cyprus, Turkey, Greece, Croatia, Albania, Montenegro, Italy and Malta and survived. Maybe it's contentment?

I can always thank plain good luck for that survival and to some degree luck did play a part, as did my experience as a motor mechanic. *But*, to me the secret of survival has been to react to the bad times with a 'calmness' which I find difficult to explain. The champion round-the-world solo sailors have it and the crews on the *'mad'* yachts racing around the world in, say, the Volvo Ocean Race, have it too.

In my view, such 'calmness' comes from experience. It's not something you can buy off-the-shelf. Why do Yacht Clubs have Junior Yacht Clubs? Why do trades have apprentices? I was an apprentice Automotive Engineer, over a five year term, and trained to do a vast range of specialised motor vehicle repairs. Eventually, because of the monotonous repetition of these repairs, the apprentice will be able to perform them with ease and a high degree of skill.

... Give the long distance stuff a go but don't forget to add a little common-sense ... it really isn't that hard"!

The same applies to managing a yacht. An *apprentice sailor* learns how to carry-out the multitude of tasks required moving a yacht efficiently by monotonous repetition. This takes a great deal of time – months and years of working on a yacht.

I had a friend visit me on DJV whilst sailing around Thailand and he had never sailed before, although he had a private pilot's licence. Obviously very interested in how a yacht is handled during the 24 hours he was aboard my friend dashed from one end of DJV to the other noting all my activities aimed at making the six tonne catamaran sail successfully. On the leg from PhiPhi Don to Phuket, a freak bit of luck found us with a fifteen knot breeze from the north. DJV just loves this strength of breeze and it was broad-side on, a beam-reach, just perfect and very rare in Asia. DJV creamed along at seven to eight knots on fairly flat water and it made sailing look *'just too simple'*.

At the end of his twenty four hour stay on board my friend's award-winning quote was: *"Now I have grasped the basics of sailing"!*
I thought to myself, "I don't think so chum", knowing full well that making it look easy had come from over 5 years at the helm!

My last word to any other would-be long distance cruising hopefuls is an encouraging one - "get out there, sail as many miles as you possibly can

You are very welcome to visit my Website at: www.svdejavu.com to check on a great volume of description and hundreds of images of my life on-board from 2004.

to build up experience, then give the long distance stuff a go but don't forget to add a little common-sense ... it really isn't that hard"!

CHAPTER 1

PREPARATIONS FOR MALAYSIA TO THE MEDITERRANEAN ... 2008 to 2010

An unknown number of sailing vessels climb over the eastern horizon of the Pacific Ocean, often through the Panama Canal and via the Galapagos Islands, sweep through the South Pacific Islands on their way to New Zealand and Australia. If they don't upset Australian Officials too much (Aussie Officials having a *black* reputation for welcoming overseas yachting visitors) they may stay for a few weeks or a few years. Then it's a natural progression for most of these sailors to sail through Indonesia *(never stopping there too long because of corruption)* and on to Singapore, Malaysia and Thailand.

Not many stay in Singapore for long unless major vessel problems dictate it, as it's expensive. If yachties want an extended stay in this area they berth across the narrow stretch of water between Singapore and Malaysia at Puteri Harbor Marina, or Danga Bay Marina, both in the area of Johor Bahru, Malaysia.

Malaysia and Thailand are a different kettle-of-fish altogether. These countries make it easy for foreign vessels and crews to stay almost indefinitely and why not. For international visitors, these countries are cheap to live in, the people friendly and climate warm. For Malaysia and Thailand it means a large amount of foreign currency deposited with all sorts of local businesses, with all the obvious benefits.

Many yachts will stay here 2-4 years and longer, while a sizeable number will be swept back East, almost as though an ebb tide has seized them, returning usually via Borneo and the Philippines, across the north of Papua New Guinea, to Australia. Not surprisingly, most are Australians or Kiwis.

But every year, like migrating ducks, approximately 100 vessels and crew are hypnotized by the challenge of sailing through to the *Mediterranean Sea*, via the Red Sea. For me this hypnotic process started early in 2007 when I spent a small fortune *(AU$6,000.00)* on a new iCOM IC-M710 high frequency (HF) radio whilst berthed at Gladstone, Queensland, Australia. This instrument made it possible to connect me to 'Sailmail', a wireless system useable while sailing thousands of miles out in the open ocean. Sailmail was developed by cruising sailors and its home is in the US. With HF radio one can connect to one of many 'home' bases around the world, all dedicated to the Sailmail system.

Once in Malaysia, Thailand and Borneo, "Where will you go from here?" became a natural talking point amongst Yachties.

The on-board Sailmail operating system resides in one's computer and connects to the HF radio via a modem. When connected, sending and receiving emails from most points around the world is a *piece-of-cake,* as we say in Australia. You don't have to be too bright to work out how satisfying this can be for people at sea ... and it's an additional safety mechanism a sailor can rely on.

The idea of sailing westwards for me had been further fanned by saying farewell to others embarking on the challenge. Once in Malaysia, Thailand and Borneo, *"Where will you go from here?"* became a natural talking point amongst yachties. Really, there's a choice of only two directions - east or west. Therefore, without thinking too much about it, I started planning what was needed for such a journey. The primary requirements would be a sturdy, reliable ship which I already possessed in the Seawind 1000 and something I didn't yet have, a skilled crew member to help.

NEW YAMAHA MOTORS FOR DÉJÀ VU ...
NOVEMBER 2009
RAFFLES MARINA, SINGAPORE
Lat: 01° 20'35N, Long: 103° 38'03E (Raffles)

Déjà vu III *(hereafter referred to as DJV)* is powered mechanically, by two 9.9hp 4 stroke, Yamaha outboard motors. Not a lot of power really. I remember well a conversation with a Yamaha mechanic in Tasmania, Australia, during my sailing visit there in 2006 when he stated with confidence, "9.9hp 4 stroke Yamaha motors have a life expectancy of 3,500 hours". He should have known, as he serviced a large fleet of fishing boats using that motor. "Change the engine oils every 100 hours and the gearbox oil every 300 hours and the life can be extended", was his good advice. Therefore, at each engine oil-change, these 'life expectancy' figures would pop back into my mind and early in 2009, my motors had reached 3,500 hours. So, a decision had to be made; if I was serious about a Malaysia to Mediterranean journey (M2M) it was vital to replace the two engines - a significant budgetary worry!

Biting the bullet, from my base in Borneo I started emailing the Yamaha dealer in Singapore, Supratechincs P/L. This is where the magic of the 'Sailmail' system helps so much when you are cruising. The model of engines I wanted were not in stock and the only way they could be supplied was via a special order which they would place with Yamaha, Japan. Prior to this happening a 40% deposit was required and the delivery time would be four months! **Bloody hell,** that seemed to me to be poor service by Yamaha, that a company as large as this wouldn't have all models in stock. I could have bought two 15 HP Honda outboards off the shelf, but I wanted to stay with the original specifications of the Seawind 1000 yacht and I decided to go for it, *a decision I was later to regret.*

So, eventually, back to Singapore from Borneo with the expectation of being greeted by two brand new 9.9hp Yamaha motors. *Wrong,* they still hadn't arrived, "Bugger and damn!" It was now four months one week since the order was placed but one week later saw them in my possession – phew!

Along with the motors came two remote controls for throttle and gear changes and two 12 litre fuel tanks. I sold the unwanted remote controls in Langkawi for AU$97.00 each and traded the 12 litre tanks with the Yamaha Dealer, Singapore, for 2 X 24 litre tanks, a changeover cost of AU$39.00 each. Good value. These tanks became my primary fuel tanks on the *M2M* run, for they were on deck and easy to refill, compared to the two main 50 litre tanks under the floor below the cockpit table.

Now for the fitting of the new motors ... *gulp!* I had the old motors out and on deck already and was confident I could fit the new motors onto the tilting holding brackets. But the electronics had me very worried. I spoke to the service manager of Supratechnics P/L to ask if he could help with the installation of the electronics. He said he would come and look at the job and promised delivery of the motors and skilled help to the Raffles Marina the following morning. This duly happened with the two motors and two mechanics arriving, on time as promised. These two men/lads *(the Singaporeans look so young!)* took over the fitting job completely and before I knew it, the motors were unboxed and installed onto the brackets, gearbox/throttle cables attached, two new Yamaha fuel filters installed and all electronics connected. It took them two days and I let them have full control ...bugger the expense, this was too important!

"The fitting charge is Compliments of Supratechnics P/L ... because you bought the motors from us!"

Upper - New engines in boxes straight from Yamaha, Japan
Centre - New engine unpacked.
Lower - Mechanics doing their job.

The motors were chirping like two happy canaries when they had finished, very quiet and smooth compared to the 'loose' old motors.

So, the time came to settle my account! I looked at the bill but there was no mention of the charge for the mechanics' labour. I asked in trepidation - "What will the labour charge be for fitting the motors"? The accounts person went away to look into this. On her return she said, *"The fitting charge is compliments of Supratechnics P/L ... because you bought the motors from us!"*

I felt a little light-headed as I was braced for at least an AU$1,000.00 bill! "Are you sure?" I asked. "Yes, that's the situation," she replied and "could we run you back to the Raffles Marina?" I felt as though I had won the Lottery. I have never experienced this sort of generosity in Australia. *Wow and wow again!*

SINGAPORE TO LANGKAWI ... 15ᵀᴴ - 30ᵀᴴ DECEMBER 2009

On leaving Singapore on the 15ᵗʰ December, 2009, DJV must have looked peculiar with two new motors humming away and two old motors strapped to the barbecue crossbar *(these I eventually sold to a used marine equipment business in Langkawi for AU$1,370, a good off-set against the cost of the new engines)*. Sailing along, I wore a broader smile as my confidence had strengthened ... it seemed DJV was ready for the Mediterranean

Sometimes, you've just got to work hard at being lucky.

A SAILING ODYSSEY - Malaysia to the Mediterranean

Upper - Both old engines stowed for carriage to Langkawi Island and resale.
Lower - Déjà vu in position at Raffles Marina, Singapore having new engines fitted.

trip when ... **Baaaang** ... the radar dome support post broke in half and the dome crashed to the deck. All of a sudden, I didn't feel so prepared! Six months before an engineer in Langkawi had made the post for me but I could now see that he had done so using 1mm thick stainless steel tubing, the type used for balustrading and decorative work not requiring weight-supporting abilities. I would need to get another one made and put it on my to-do-list for when I got to Penang.

Whilst wrapping the radar dome in sticky clear wrap I noticed the top cover of the dome missing. As the saying goes "Shit happens" but I knew it would take ages and many dollars to get a new one. Being an optimist I turned DJV around and motored back along our 'snail-trail' on the chart-plotter. About a mile back, what should I spot floating top side down, but the cover? *Sometimes, you've just got to work hard at being lucky.*

It was now time to 'skip' 420 nmiles north, along the west coast of Malaysia via Malacca, Port Dickson *(where I was caught in a cyclonic storm which tore the mainsail)* Pankcol Island *(where, in 2009, DJV was rammed by a steel 60 by 15 metre, rock-carrying barge)* and Penang to get to Langkawi as quickly as possible. I now had an additional problem to rectify ... one torn mainsail. Through the yachty network I learnt of a woman called A'rea in Langkawi very capable of repairing sails so, I headed straight for her. She was a small woman, Finnish born and a US citizen and she took the job willingly. The only downside was it would be mid-January before completion of the repair.

A SAILING ODYSSEY-Malaysia to the Mediterranean

Upper left - Six month old radar post snapping ... again around Port Dickson.
Upper right - Beverly helping sail maker.
Lower - Sail torn in mini-hurricane off Port Dickson, Malaysia

I arrived in Penang on 24th December 2009 all set to celebrate Christmas. I had known good friends, Patrick and Elizabeth, *SV Labarque*, were stuck in a grubby little ship building yard on the SE corner of Penang and I had been communicating with them about their plans for Xmas Day and asked if I could join them. "No worries", was the reply and I therefore anchored DJV out from the shipyard and motored ashore by dinghy. It was a stinking hot day and the hull of their yacht, made of steel, was a perfect magnet for retaining the heat. Inside was like an oven and I had brought ice-cream and plum pudding for Xmas Day lunch desert and I found out too late they didn't have a fridge. We therefore enjoyed plum pudding with liquid ice-cream. Some things in life are just not meant to be!

Penang has one of the few offices in Malaysia (outside of Kuala Lumpur) able to issue a visa for India and given the warning this would be a very lengthy process, I wanted to get on with it. Having applied on the 28th December I learnt I could pick up the visa on a return run early in 2010, an easy journey as Penang Island is just 80 nmiles south of Langkawi.

1ST MATE BEVERLY PEARSON ... CANADIAN

My priority now was to sail to Langkawi in time to pick up my, as yet unmet 1st-mate-to-be, Beverly Pearson who was flying from Canada to sail with DJV and due to arrive on the 1st January 2010. It had been obvious to me I should have at least one other person on-board for this journey for all sorts of reasons but primarily so I could sleep safely whilst travelling waters such as the Indian Ocean and Arabian Sea where there would be many large, fast-moving ships. There have been many who have done such a journey solo which would have been my fall-back situation if I had had a ***huge*** amount of problems finding a 1st mate. As a solo sailor, in order to get any rest at all, you just have to sail well away from the known shipping lanes and using two alarms, wake yourself up regularly to check for vessels of all sizes and speeds. Whilst asleep, solo, you are in the hands of the God Poseidon!! **Risky!**

My approach to locating a crew member had been to join the internet site 'Find-a-Crew'. Finding crew 'off-the-street' *(in harbours)* sometimes happens but it hadn't happened for me on this trip. All the local cruising fraternity knew I was sailing west and had there been anyone available, keen and capable they would have made themselves known, hence my joining 'Find-a-Crew'. This is ***not*** a crew agency system - their network is designed to help you independently find a good crew, or alternatively, a great boat to join, which provides a cheaper and faster alternative to an agency. Find-a-Crew is suited to people who like to make their own decisions about what's best for them. It operates on a database system which requires information from a ship/yacht owner such as vessel type, details of proposed journey and so on.

Beverly, from the cold-lands of Canada was the end product of the Find-a-Crew system and proved ideal.

The prospective crew also become a member *(it's free to them and to the skippers)*. Find-a-Crew makes their money from offering 'premium' membership as 'free' membership exchanges only very basic information between members. Prospective crew then enter their 'dream-list' of where they would like to sail and when. The system crunches the two lots of information and in some magical way marries them together, then sends information about potential crew that may seem acceptable, back to the skipper. Skippers then vet the applications and reply to those they feel could be compatible with them and the task. I found many people applying who seemed not-to-be-on-this-planet, who were 'time-wasters' or just 'dreamers'. I nevertheless replied to them all.

Although I had intimated I would consider a male crew member, I didn't seriously vet applications from men. History has convinced me I get along much better with a female crew than with male. I prefer women because: (a) They usually talk a language I can understand (not football, soccer and rugby talk). (b) Women tend to be more curious and interested in what's going on around them. (c) They tend to be more capable in the galley. (d) I find they are usually prettier than men **and** (e) The women I invite aboard are always interested in sailing!

Beverly, from the cold-lands of Canada was the end product of the Find-a-Crew system and proved ideal. She had experience of crewing a racing yacht out of Hong Kong to the Philippines and had raced around the lakes of Toronto, Canada. Beverly and I had spoken for some time by 'phone in a mutual interview

Beverly after recovering from 35 hour journey from Canada.

process and seemed to get along well enough. I guessed if we had trouble talking over a 'phone there wouldn't be much chance we would communicate well face-to-face.

It's difficult to know how to handle selecting a stranger to travel with when you can't meet this person face-to-face. I remember meeting my editor for this book for the very first time in Brunei; she was interested in sailing/racing with me on DJV from Miri to Kota Kinabalu. She and her husband knew nothing about me so invited me to dinner which provided an opportunity to do some mutual face-to-face checking-out of experience, expertise, attitude and personality. But that was only a 4 day trip and Beverley and I would be together for six months, much more of a gamble.

Besides our phone calls, Beverly also requested to talk to other women who had crewed for me. I guess she wanted to get a sense of any risk involved, what sort of sailor I was, but also what kind of person I was and whether she would be safe with me in more personal ways, for example whether I showed traits of being a drunkard, or, maybe a serial, sexual maniac! Having done this sizing up, we decided to go for it and ended up with a near perfect match from both sides *(well that's what I think)!*

Beverly arrived at Langkawi Airport, Malaysia, Friday 1st January 2010 in 35°C heat, after a 35 hour journey from Toronto, Canada, which had been buried in ice and snow with a temperature of -20°C. To say she took the temperature difference in her stride is a gross understatement. After a one day and night sleep Bev was straight into her bikinis showing off her glaring white complexion for the sun to start work on. And better still she was ready for work and we had lots to do -

- Visit computer whiz, Vennie, to have him replace a battery charger and fit 'MaxSea' to both my computers. 'MaxSea' is an electronic navigation system and was to prove a God-send later in our journey.
- To buy an orbital sander with which to polish DJV.
- To call on our sail maker, A'rea.
- To buy courtesy flags for the countries we were to visit. It's protocol to fly a small courtesy flag of the country you are visiting on entering their waters. It is usually flown half way up the mast and should be larger than the home flag you are flying.
- Beverly bought about 20 paper charts as she was keen to plot our course as we went along ... which she did.
- Beach DJV to clean hulls.
- Return to Penang for the Indian visa and new radar post.
- Fill all containers with fuel.
- Same re water.
- Buy and store half-a-tonne of food.
- Fit new CD/AM/FM player.
- Fit new VHF radio.
- Wait for 'Spinlock' deck clutch parts from Australia.
- Plus a thousand other things!

Upper - DJV on the beach of Telaga Harbour, Langkawi, Malaysia.
Lower - Beverly enjoying the warm waters of Malaysia.

Beverly came on-board a quite stressed, unhappy person. She was in the throes of a divorce and had a much-loved 17 year old son just starting university. She therefore had the challenge of managing these events by remote control. You might think this would have been a bad time to have taken off on an international long-term sailing journey but, in Beverly's case, I feel the diversion was helpful. With 'Sailmail' on-board Beverly had excellent email communications with the outside world, almost anywhere we were sailing and this relieved a lot of her personal pressure.

Beverly brought many skills as 1st Mate; she was familiar with yachts and the many controls for sails, anchors etc., she wasn't subject to the woes of seasickness and she was fearless when *'push-came-to-shove'* (such as climbing on-board a three metre diameter floating, seagull-splattered, shipping buoy in the harbour of Al Mukalla, Yemen, at 03:00 in the morning ... or being hauled to the top of the mast).

REPAIRS AND PROVISIONING OF DJV ... 1ST TO 27TH JANUARY 2010
KUAH, LANGKAWI, MALAYSIA
Lat: 06° 18'53E, Long: 099° 50'36E (Kuah)

Before we returned to Penang to pick up the radar post, we decided it was prudent to beach DJV on a small island adjacent to Telaga Harbour, Langkawi, Malaysia. Therefore, just after high tide we nudged onto the beach, having set a stern anchor well out and for'ard mooring lines to a tree stump on the beach and waited for low tide. I had done this several times before on this beach, so I was confident. With DJV hard aground at low tide Bev and I then enjoyed the task of scraping barnacles from the hulls and giving DJV a good polishing. This could be done wearing bathers, with a swim every 10 minutes to keep the blood temperature down. Beverly enjoyed this, particularly given the two metre snow drifts she had just come from.

That done, we re-floated the next day at high-tide and took off back to Kuah, the capital of Langkawi Island where we had been advised the mainsail was ready for pickup. My Finnish/US friend wasn't cheap at AU$286.00, but, she can afford to be expensive, having a monopoly on the business in this area. I'm not complaining as the job looked great under sail. Again Bev proved a great asset as the sail is huge, heavy and difficult to re-fit to DJV on your own.

So off to Penang to pick up a visa for India and to have the new radar post fitted. We would be mooring in Penang City Marina, which I knew from previous experiences was ***designed in hell*** with its disco in the centre of the marina and the cyclonic-like swell and currents from the nearby ferry terminal rushing through the marina. Penang was 80nmiles south and this would be a good time to see what Bev could do as 1st mate. The first morning out

> *DJV was travelling at 6 knots which equates to 3.08 metres every second - how long does it take for anything that falls overboard to disappear from sight? Not long at all!*

> *We met with Patrick and Elizabeth of SV Labarque still stuck in the crummy shipyard. By that time, they had been cruising for 20 years, covering over 100,000 nmiles.*

from Langkawi ... *I lost her;* she was nowhere to be seen! Surely this couldn't be possible? With much shouting on my part I was rewarded with a reply from Beverly who was dragging her feet through the water whilst sitting on the lower step on the port side hull of DJV enjoying the warm water and the beautiful conditions. I had to have a 'quiet' chat to her about that as one slip could find her overboard. *And* if the Skipper wasn't close at hand to hear or see this occur she could be lost forever. DJV was travelling at 6 knots which equates to 3.08 metres every second - how long does it take for anything/anyone that falls overboard to disappear from sight? I can tell you - *not many seconds at all!*

We docked in the Penang City Marina and nothing had changed, the disco was still there as loud as ever and at my suggestion Beverly elected to stay in a hotel for one of the nights. After two days, the new radar post arrived. It had been made from 3mm thick stainless steel and has been a stout ally since. Cost for the new post was AU$179.00, half that of the original 'look good' post which had snapped.

During our time in Penang, we met with Patrick and Elizabeth of *SV Labarque* still stuck in the crummy shipyard. By this time, they had been cruising for

20 years, covering over 100,000 nmiles. Here were a very private couple, whom I had first met during the 2007 Sail Indonesia Rally out of Darwin, Northern Territory, Australia. From the UK, these two were true 'blue-water sailors' on a yacht which was, by their own admission, one of the slowest on the planet. But they clearly had the time, patience and energy to stick at it. Like many other yachties I had met, they had invested most of their money in their yacht and lived quite simply, travelling the world for years on end wherever the fancy took them and always glad to meet up with friends *(as we had done at Christmas)* made on earlier yachting encounters.

We picked up the visa for India and visited the huge Penang supermarket to buy further provisions for the trip. Although I had spoken to a few crews who had done long distant cruising I wasn't too scientific about provisioning. Beverly and I decided we needed:

- As much fruit and vegetables as we could carry and eat, before it went off. The Seawind 1000 has the greatest freezer/fridge in the world, not huge but very handy and this freezer was packed with frozen meat.
- Lots of baked beans, beer and coke.
- Long life milk and milk powder.
- Plenty of Vegemite (an Australian version of Marmite) which makes a great soup; and the Canadian would soon adapt when she got hungry enough wouldn't she?
- And a thousand other goods.

Beverly guarding some of the provisions purchased for the M2M journey.

The Seawind 1000 carries 400 litres of drinking water in its main tank ... and I had another eighty litres in plastic containers. This vessel had been fitted with a power pump that lifted salt water to one of the dish-washing troughs in the galley; the practice being to wash dirty dishes in salt water (with detergent) and then rinse in freshwater, thereby saving on fresh water. ***A good system that works!***

> *Then disaster struck, again; about two miles south of Langkawi, at 23:00 in pitch darkness, with DJV doing eight knots, we hit something very, very heavy and hard with the starboard hull.*

I didn't keep tabs on the weight and cost of all the provisions but it was significant. Throughout the journey, however, we found we were able to replenish our food larder at almost all stop-overs.

We left Penang at 1300, on the 15th January 2010 heading back to Langkawi. The ride back was fast and furious *(NNE winds to 30 knots)* propelling DJV along at 5-8 knots. She averaged 6 knots for this trip which is very good for her. ***Then disaster struck, again;*** about two miles south of Langkawi, at 23:00 in pitch darkness, with DJV doing eight knots, we hit something very, very heavy and hard with the starboard hull. It felt like a log as it stood DJV on her nose while whatever it was swept under the starboard hull. Damage report

A SAILING ODYSSEY-Malaysia to the Mediterranean

Upper - From restaurant on Koh Lipe Island, Butang Group, Thailand.
Centre - Beach camping visitors to DJV ... L-R 'Kip', 'Beverly', 'Isabel' and 'Lloyd'
Lower - Local boats conveying tourists around islands ... Koh Lipe Island.

- a paddle wheel (which registers water speed past the hull) was smashed. ***"Bugger and bugger again!"!*** We didn't have the time to fix it (a new assembly being required) but I decided we could leave without it, as its absence was not life-threatening.

Once back in Langkawi waiting for more spare parts, we had time for some R and R ... with a visit from Roger Manning, a friend of mine from Sydney, Australia and a trip to the Butang Group of Islands, part of Thailand, about 28 nmiles WNW of Langkawi. This was a bonus for Bev and me as we may never sail in Thai waters again. We enjoyed the crystal clear waters immensely and made two new young friends who were camping on a beach near our anchorage.

Back to Langkawi as it was now the 25th January 2010 and I wasn't going to leave any later than the end of the month. We re-filled DJV with fuel and water, spent all my remaining Malay Ringgits on food and at 16:30 on the 27th January, 2010, DJV left Langkawi for the last time and we were off on our odyssey, heading roughly west for Aceh in Indonesia, 238 nmiles away.

Chapter 2

LANGKAWI, MALAYSIA TO ACEH, INDONESIA ... FROM 27TH JANUARY 2010

Movement west along the channel from Kuah, Langkawi was slow but eventually we came adjacent to the international cruise ship terminal and were gladdened by the beautiful sight of the sailing cruise ship, *'SV Star Clipper'* preparing to leave the terminal. She is a three-masted, true sailing vessel and the Captain's specialty is to raise all sails on leaving port and have display lights glowing. Magnificent!

I set DJV on a direct course for the northern end of Aceh, Indonesia, 283 nmiles away. I hadn't sought an Indonesian cruising permit (known as a CAIT) for this stopover as yachtsmen who had used these moorings advised it was a safe bet to call in un-officially. *Gulp*. Indonesian officials are renowned for dealing harshly with interlopers to their country. Permits are a real pain to obtain though and expensive, so I relied on others' advice to stop here without a CAIT and all was OK as promised.

DJV was heavily laden with half a tonne of water and equal weight of fuel, a heap of food and all the hundred other things you must have for such a journey

Upper - Four Mast Cruise Ship 'Star Clipper' getting under way from Langkawi, Malaysia
Centre - At anchor in channel at Aceh, Indonesia.
Lower - Skipper in rescue mode for Bev being swept away by strong current.

(plus, Beverly's baggage which defied my attempt to lift aboard - just joking).

DJV surprised me with the speed and agility she displayed through the first night. With a 15 knot ESE'er she was moving at 5-7.5 knots and due to the weight she was carrying I decided to put an extra reef in the mainsail. I'm sure we had the help of a current moving in our direction.

SHIP'S LOG:

I had set-up a 'ship's log' manual to record our daily experiences and diligently made entries on a six hour routine with information such as:

- Date/hour
- Latitude/Longitude
- Odometer Reading
- Distance to Destination ... ETA
- Heading
- Wind Direction
- Wind Speed (True)
- Speed over the Ground
- Journey duration to date
- Ambient temperature
- Comments (On anything unusual ... tidal waves, chart plotter failure etc.)

On completing the journey and for confirming facts for the writing of this book, the log was invaluable. Mind you at 0600 in the morning after a tedious night on watch you had to wonder if it was worth it. *Yes it was!*

Through the following day we started to encounter heavy movements of large ships proving to be the single biggest threat to sailing this route. Shipping movement into and out of the Straits of Malacca is huge due in the main to Singapore being the main hub for the dispersal of container and other cargo. The shipping is thick and fast with most ships cruising above 20 knots. This means a ship may not be visible on the horizon, but, 20 minutes later could be running you down. Because of this, it's vital to have radar. Beverly was a very good lookout and soon gained the nickname 'Radar' herself, as nothing moved on a 360° horizon around us that Bev didn't see. I stressed with her, however, that she was to wake me for the slightest anxiety she had about what was going on around us and this she did.

With the breeze dropping to 4 knots it was time to drop the mainsail and fire up one of the motors. I adopted a policy of not cruising with more than one motor running at any one time for fuel conservation reasons; we had a long, long way to go. Beverly was finding it hard to settle into the 'watch' routine but it was early days and we were tired from the preparation of DJV. I decided to have a short R & R stopover in Pulau We, Aceh, Indonesia and hooked

> *Finding a mooring buoy in the dark is a challenge and my tip to anyone in this situation is to use your 'daytime' binoculars ...*

Upper - Lloyd entering data to log every six hours.
Lower - Shipping going into and coming out of the Straits of Malacca, Malaysia.

onto a mooring buoy at 03:00 on the 30th January 2010. Finding a mooring buoy in the dark is a challenge and my tip to anyone in this situation is to use your 'daytime' binoculars as they magnify the available light enormously.

This area was devastated by the Tsunami of 2004

We had travelled;

- 283 nmiles from Langkawi in 58 hours
- An average speed of 4.8 knots per hour.

PULAU WE, ACEH, INDONESIA,
Lat: 05°52.68N, Long: 095°15.44E (Aceh)

Pulau We is a small scattered village with a couple of 'would-be' stores and restaurants catering to the back-packer tourist interested in snorkelling, deep sea diving and escaping from the outside world and a very good place it is to do such a thing. The water was crystal clear and a strong current ran through our anchorage. Beverly took a swim as it was 30°C with 95% humidity and despite wearing fins was swept away with the current. Skipper to the rescue with the inflatable dinghy.

This area was devastated by the Tsunami of 2004 and a monument of thanks is displayed near the town centre to the Canadians who had supported the area financially and practically - helping with cleaning and restoration. We enjoyed this stay but come 07:00 Monday 1st February, 2010, it was time to move further west.

Chapter 3

ACEH, INDONESIA TO GALLE, SRI LANKA ... FROM 1ST FEBRUARY 2010.

From Aceh, Sri Lanka is approximately 1,000 nmile west across the Indian Ocean. DJV averaged 5.2 knots on this leg, assisted by a strong westerly current, a good average speed for this little girl.

Bev was on-watch from noon 'til 18:00. I had borrowed a watch schedule from the Argentinean Navy for craft with two crew members:

- Beverly-   noon 'til 18:00;
- Lloyd-   18:00 'til midnight;
- Beverly-   midnight 'til 04:00;
- Lloyd-   04:00 'til 08:00;
- Beverly-   08:00 'til 10:00;
- Lloyd-   10:00 'til noon.

And then we would start all over again. It soon became obvious this roster did not suit Bev at all as she wasn't able to rest properly during her time off, so we changed to four hours on four hours off, which seemed much better.

Around 14:30 Bev called down to me, "Come and have a look at something". Up I bounded (as

> *I took a closer look and then another and became convinced it was a rolling tidal-wave heading our way ...*

I was still refreshed from Aceh) to hear Bev's concern regarding our possible collision course with a ship on our starboard side coming out of the Straits of Malacca and travelling fast. This was exactly the sort of reason I had explained to Bev that I wished to be called if she was anxious about anything. We studied the radar together and I made some observations explaining why we were in a good position to clear this ship safely and taught Bev the *'are-we-going-to-collide'* formula (see Glossary). The incident was therefore a worthwhile lesson.

Then scanning around as one normally does when on deck, to my surprise, on the western horizon as far as I could see from left to right, it looked as though a boiling white, storm-like, lather had developed. It seemed unlikely in this weather, so I asked Bev if she had looked at this **phenomenon.** "Where are the bino's (binoculars) Beverly?" I took a closer look and then another and I was willing to bet **two-bob-to-a-pinch-of-possum-shit** it was a rolling tidal-wave heading our way – this was something very new to me. Should I tell Bev as it may panic her? Well, she would know about it very soon so why not. "Have a look Beverly; I think we have a tidal wave heading our way." I think I heard a Canadian expletive from Beverly *("I think we're screwed Lloyd")* but I was busy scanning the radar. Across the entire screen was a solid line and it was travelling toward us *fast*.

"Beverly" ...

- "Into our life jackets";
- "Close all hatches";
- "Drop the sails";
- "Fire up the two engines";
- "Put our 'wash boards' in place" (they are a flat fiberglass board which seals off each hull from entry, usually from pirates and thieves but a tidal wave is a good enough reason);
- "Unclip the 'EPIRB' and tie it to the side rail"; (an EPIRB is an electronic device, now mandatory to have onboard in Australia which, when activated by a switch, sends out a signal of your position in latitude and longitude to a satellite, which in turn redirects the signal to a ground emergency station in Australia, who arranges for someone - a ship in our situation - to divert to your position).

And I don't mean it to sound as though I made Bev do all the work, just most of it.

"Beverly, what I propose to do is turn and run parallel with the wave and when it is close, turn into it with both engines running as hard as possible. We will try to climb over it." *The scary part was I had no idea how high the wave was as radar will not convey this information. It could be one metre, or, it could be five metres?* Having got organised, I had time then to do a calculation from what we could see on the radar screen. We picked the wave up when it was about 10 nmiles from us and it took 15 minutes to reach us. It was travelling across the surface at 40+ nmiles per hour.

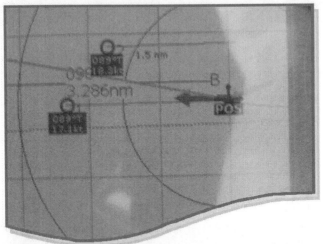

Upper - Tidal wave (1500mm high) passing under DJV
Centre - Radar image of two freighters powering towards DJV.
Lower - One of the ships passing down the port side.

We were very anxious, if not terrified, about this *'thing'*. You could see the froth from the wave moving closer, very quickly and then it was on us ... but thank goodness, it was only about 1½ metres high and spiky. DJV wasn't at all fazed; she just stuck her bows into it and chopped her way through. She took a lot of water over the bows and foredeck which cascaded down each side of the cockpit, but, with the high buoyancy at the bows, despite our huge weight on board, pencilled through and lifted above the chop. And that's what it was, a severe, spiky chop, much like a wind-against-current chop and a few seconds later it was behind us. *Wow!*

We agreed this phenomenon would have been a very nasty scare at night, as you wouldn't pick it up unless alerted by radar. Then, what on earth would you think it was? It would have been an experience a hundred times more terrifying. Another thought came to us that maybe it was a repeat of the infamous and tragic Tsunami of December, 2004. Later, we made enquiries through our on-board *Sailmail* email system but, luckily, no Tsunamis had devastated Asia. I've had a few real scares on my journey and this rates close to the top of the list.

For our first 24 hours out of Aceh, DJV had travelled 152 nmiles at an average

> *"I think we're going to be squashed-like-a-bug, Lloyd, what shall we do?" "We don't have a choice Beverly, we'll 'thread-the-needle' and go between them*

speed of 6.3 knots with a strong westerly current in our favour. 753 nmiles to go to Sri Lanka.

The following morning I had a call from Bev, again on watch – she needed me to look at something. About five miles ahead of us were two huge freighters about half a mile apart (that's very close by shipping standards especially with them being side-by-side and going so fast) both travelling straight at us at 18 knots. Bev had worked out she could not cross either of their paths in time to let them go by. "I think we're going to be squashed-like-a-bug, Lloyd, what shall we do?" "We don't have a choice Beverly, we'll 'thread-the-needle' *and* go between them", I replied. From a distance it seemed an impossible gap between these giants but, adjacent to them, we could see there was plenty of room for our six metre beam and we carried on through, knowing we could manoeuvre quickly enough to avoid either ship.

I wondered what had been going on on the bridges of these two ships. Were they mates having a race? Or, maybe they were mates wanting to give this yacht the scare of its life. Maybe both ships were on 'auto-pilot' and didn't realise they were so close to one another? *I seriously don't think so though!*

Soon after noon, the seas started to rise, with the wind speed increasing to 17 knots and blowing from the NE

We later heard during this weather a friend sailing west of Sri Lanka to the Maldives, had lost a mast and motored back to Galle, Sri Lanka.

and I turned DJV 10° off the wind to smooth our ride a bit. We had three reefs in the main and the small jib flying and appeared to be north of the main shipping movements so our sightings of shipping reduced.

On our 3rd day out of Aceh we saw little shipping at all. We were definitely north of the main shipping channel (Latitude: 06°13' 00N, Longitude: 088° 12'12E) with squalls coming through, forcing us to put a fourth reef in the main. We were still doing 5.3 knots. The end of our 3rd day out of Aceh we had travelled 126 nmiles at an average of 5.25 knots/p/h. DJV was 477 nmiles from Sri Lanka.

Our next day was a combination of 8-10 knot winds and DJV was making quiet progress but eventually the wind calmed off completely. Time to fire up one of the Yamaha outboards. The end of the 4th day out from Aceh we travelled 115 nmiles at an average speed of 4.8 knots/p/h. We were still making good progress with 363 nmiles to go to Sri Lanka.

The 5th day out from Aceh found the wind picking up from the NE with seas getting rough and I had a headache, probably from too little water intake and lack of rest. It was hot. At midnight we were 270 nmiles from Galle, Sri Lanka with winds having strengthened to 25 knots and turning to NNW. The seas were building. I had

> *A few minute before my watch at midnight, Bev called down "Lloyd, our auto-pilot has crashed." Why do all the fun things happen while Beverly's on duty?*

Top left - Auto pilot drive assembly ... failed two days out from Sri Lanka. We had a new unit in reserve!
Top right - Bev's not praying, just talking to the dolphins.
Centre - A common occurrence of tired passengers staying for a night.
Bottom - Not-so-friendly looking patrol boat at entrance to Galle, Sri Lanka harbour.

to bear DJV away south again, as it was impossible to keep our heading to the SE shoreline of Sri Lanka. DJV was taking a heavy pounding, as was the crew. *(We later heard during this weather a friend sailing west of Sri Lanka to the Maldives (SV Meridian) had lost a mast and had to motor back to Galle, Sri Lanka.)* It was incredible how the hulls and everything else on DJV could sustain the bone-jarring hammering of these fast moving waves, hour after hour for two and a half days. The entire boat was working very hard, especially the auto-pilot. And for the crew it was impossible to rest.

The 5th day out from Aceh we travelled 142 nmiles at an average speed of 5.9 knots and were still 227 nmiles from Galle, Sri Lanka. Strong winds of 25/35 knots continued with the 'fetch' *(the distance across the water from a solid object directly upwind, in this case the shores of NE India in the Bay of Bengal, to DJV)* being 1,000 nmiles. These strong winds and long 'fetch' meant tall, fast moving waves were slamming DJV mercilessly.

A few minute before my watch at midnight, Bev called down *"Lloooooyd, our auto-pilot has crashed."* Why do all the fun things happen while Beverly's on duty? *"Shit and disaster, this could be serious"*. From experience over the six years I had been sailing, I knew the auto-pilot was one of my greatest and hardest-working allies. The faster the Seawind 1000 went and the rougher the water, the harder the auto-pilot had to work. But, what a solid worker; equivalent to having an extra person on board and you didn't have to feed or rest it ... plus, no human could steer a course as straight. But, it had a finite life span and this was the third auto-pilot drive assembly I'd fitted to DJV. I had prepared for a 4th failure with a brand new spare stowed away below decks.

"Beverly you will have to steer DJV manually with the port wheel while I dismantle the starboard wheel assembly." *(Seawind 1000's having two steering wheels for just such an occasion and the second one is also very handy for docking in a marina - what a design sensation.) Why didn't I think to heave-to?* I was knackered - it had been a few days since I had had a decent rest - but this couldn't wait. It turned out to be a simple job, a-piece-of-cake. The wheel came off with the gentle persuasion of a large crescent wrench and a hammer, the old auto-pilot drive assembly came apart easily and the new assembly was unpacked and bolted into place, apparently without mishap. The only problem was it wouldn't work. Beverly to the rescue; "Lloyd there's an arrow on each half of the assembly, shouldn't they be aligned"? How had Bev noticed that in the dark and whilst steering DJV? Surely she was as tired as me? But, she was absolutely right, the two arrows weren't aligned. And with their alignment the unit started working perfectly.

"You're not the sharpest-tool-in-the-shed when you're tired, are you Skipper"! She could be so harsh!
Champagne for Beverly in Sri Lanka.
Our rough ride on the 5th day out turned into a 54 hour ordeal and the only reprieve was our arrival in the lee of the SE corner of Sri Lanka where we anchored in Matara Bay, 23 nmiles east of Galle Harbour.

Next day at 13:30 we arrived at Galle to be welcomed by a deadly looking little gunship with three machine guns mounted on the fore deck ... which seemed to be saying "Just don't try anything buster or we'll *blow-you-out-of-the-water"!* Wow, what a welcome.

We had travelled:

- 926 nmiles in just under 7.5 days
- An average speed of 5.2 knots.

I was very, very pleased with DJV and my crew.

Chapter 4

GALLE, SRI LANKA TO COCHIN, INDIA ... 13th FEBRUARY 2010
Lat: 06° 01'57N, Long: 080° 13'54E (Galle)

We left Galle in a thunderstorm, an unusual storm with great streaks of lightning and heavy rain from the north, but little wind. Progress was slow as a result even with one of the Yamahas buzzing away. *"Why leave an anchorage in a storm?"* I sense someone asking. Answer; I had decided the size and strength of this storm meant it was moving fast enough to be clear of us in a very short time and we were in the lee of a large headland. And so it turned out.

Crossing the Gulf of Mannar between Sri Lanka and the Indian continent proved a roughish journey and very slow for the first fifteen hours. The first 24 hours saw DJV move just 98 nmiles. Winds then swung to the NNE and strengthened to 16 knots and we found we were on a

> *Can you imagine the sight from the fishing boat of DJV under full sail, travelling quite fast, bearing down on you? Bloody scary stuff.*

perfect 'reach'. DJV loves sailing with the wind attacking the hull from a direction between 70° and 110° off the side of either hull, a 'broad reach'.

With 15/23 knot winds swinging between N and NE we were in a good sailing position to have DJV pull us through 126 nmiles in the next 24 hours which would be a good average for us. Significant shipping numbers moving into the Gulf of Mannar was worth watching out for. We were now 5/6 nmiles off the western coast of India, it was dark and there were hundreds of small fishing boats ahead of us, with thousands of twinkling lights showing their position and it was Beverly's watch ...

At 03:00 I heard Bev shout urgently from on deck, *"Llooooooooyddd, come quick"*. Up I dashed, bleary eyed, as there was real panic in her tone (I didn't feel I had time to wash my face) to find that DJV was sailing beautifully at 6 knots but 150 metres dead ahead was a 7 metre, open, dinghy-type fishing boat. We were about to kill all on board and destroy the boat - and we wouldn't be adding value to DJV's condition either. To make matters worse, we could see there was a smaller boat to our left trying to get back to the bigger fishing boat dead ahead. It was clear the crew on board had seen us at the last minute.

I whipped the auto-pilot lever into neutral and manually steered DJV to port around the larger vessel, missing it by inches whilst Bev screamed again, *"Watch the smaller boat on our left"*. I couldn't see it but nevertheless swung DJV violently back toward the coast, effectively doing a tight 'horse shoe' circuit around the larger boat. We didn't hit anything but we had two very shocked people on-board DJV and I was certain the fishermen were giving thanks to their God. Can you imagine the sight from the fishing boat of DJV under full sail, travelling quite fast, bearing down on you? **Bloody scary stuff.**

Beverly had been duped into *not* seeing this craft because it had its entire squid light arrangement hanging down over the side away from DJV, hence, from a distance, the vessel was just a black blob hidden in the dark. (Squid lights are usually a bunch of very bright 1000 watt quartz halogen lamps and on a small boat such as this, powered by a small benzene powered generator. I've seen larger squid boats in Indonesia shining twenty of these lamps into the sea. The squid swim up to the lights from the bottom and are usually scooped up in large nets.)

We were five miles from the coast and looking ahead and seeing thousands of bright lights, it was obvious we were going to experience many more similar situations if we kept on this course. "OK, Beverly, we'll do a 90° turn to port and head out until we're ten miles from the coast and then turn north again; can you arrange that?" And I went back to my bunk to rest.

My shift and I was aware that in the last 24 hours we had only travelled 104 nmiles. We weren't breaking any speed records and were still 70 nmiles from Cochin. At 05:00 (still dark) I noticed a large, well lit power boat about a mile off our

"Just give me a moment Beverly, there's someone here trying to kill us".

starboard bow, heading across our path. In applying the *'are-we-going-to-collide'* formula, I realised unless one of us changed course, *yes*, we were going to collide. This bastard was driving a 20 metre solid pleasure craft, not a fishing boat, travelling at 15 knots and approaching DJV at a 45° angle. And he just kept on coming. Bev came up with a cup of coffee and I remarked, *"Just give me a moment Beverly, there's someone here trying to kill us"*. I kept DJV on the collision course until this idiot was 60-80 metres away and then turned hard to starboard and slid down his port side. The maniac must have had a grudge against visiting yachts as he was definitely going to sink us. In hindsight I could only deduce this skipper was prepared to sustain damage to his own craft *(which his insurance company may have repaired)* whilst in the act of ramming DJV *(which wasn't insured)*. Maybe the vessel was on auto-pilot and there was no one on lookout? That or the skipper didn't know or didn't care about that simple 'law-of-the-sea' … that a powered vessel must always give way to a vessel under sail. We will never know and I wasn't going to stick around to argue!

We came to the entrance to Cochin Harbour and the chart-plotter showed a gaggle of shallows and obstacles. So I dropped anchor in five metres of calm water, a mile from the coast and we went down below for a well-earned rest.

Galle, Sri Lanka to Cochin, India had proved to be:

- A 365 nmiles journey taking us 81 hours
- An average speed of 4.5 knots.

COCHIN HARBOUR, INDIA ...
17ᵀᴴ FEBRUARY 2011
Lat: 09°59'06N, Long: 076°16'13E

At 10:15 on the 17th February 2010, we entered Cochin Harbour, India and after radio contact to shore, a customs officer, a very pleasant, youngish guy, immaculately dressed in a white naval uniform, came on-board. You had to quickly get used to dealing with a heap of paperwork in India (they still use carbon copy paper) and we had to wade through seven copies of a five page report (or was it five copies of a seven page report?). Either way, it was a hell-of-a-lot of paper and time for another Canadian expletive from Beverly; *"Holy Cow Batman"!*

When the on-board paperwork was complete, we were taken ashore to manoeuvre our way through customs, immigration, the harbour-master and *'The Department of Homeland Security'* (a mob looking out for terrorists I think). The British influence is thick in these offices and to see the years-old heaps of paper stacked on old desks, rotting away with the passing decades, was to observe a slice of ancient British Colonial history. We were eventually directed to an anchorage, without choice, but conveniently enough anchored amongst other visiting yachts.

> *This was the beginning of a sour relationship, as he was a drug addict. He would never know how close he came to being murdered by Beverly.*

Upper left - Fishing nets at entrance to Cochin, India harbour.
Upper right - Immaculate Customs/Immigration Officer.
Centre - Beverly with Agent ... a great worry to us.
Lower: Anchorage in Cochin harbour.

During the initial anchoring to await the visit from our Customs officer, a local wizened-looking guy had rowed alongside wanting to act as our agent. I ignored him, but he followed us ashore and while we were filling out papers, he worked on the customs officer (CO), obviously trying to 'sell' himself to us, through him. Eventually the CO turned to me and recommended this chap as a reliable agent. This was the beginning of a sour relationship, as he didn't understand a word of English and was also a drug addict who from about noon each day didn't even comprehend 'sign language'. He would never know how close he came to being murdered by Beverly.

Drinking water in 20 litre jugs was available through this agent, plus fuel and most supplies. We spent the best part of a day searching for food as he didn't seem to understand the word 'Supermarket'. Eventually, with the aid of an English-speaking friend he took us to two of the smallest convenience stores imaginable. This was the best we could find so we bought available goods to suit our needs.

I needed a haircut and mimed accordingly. He found me one and that was a success. Come time to pay I decided to tip the barber 100 Rupee (AU$2.20), which he was very pleased with. When I asked the cost of the haircut, he said 50 Rupee (AU$1.10). No wonder he was pleased with the tip. It had also been funny and as good as a play when Bev, whilst I was still in the barber's chair, asked if I would like a coffee. *"Yes please."* Ten minutes later, back came Beverly with coffee and

A SAILING ODYSSEY-Malaysia to the Mediterranean

Upper left - Bev choosing 'Muslim pleasing' gowns for further down the track.
Upper right - Haircut India style ... I tipped twice the cost of the cut!
Centre - Beverly driving us out of Cochin Harbour.
Lower - Sunset on Cochin ... Goodbye!

everything in the salon stopped while they waited for *'The King'* (me) to have his drink. I've never felt so important.

Beverly was adamant she wanted to buy a couple of sets of garments to cover her body and head in order to show respect for the Muslim culture further down the track in Oman, Yemen, Eritrea, Sudan and Egypt. She was taken to a store which offered a wide range of clothing and deliberated for an hour about what was best for the job. At truly great expense she bought two garments but later on, wearing them, concluded they must have been made from straw - they were as tough and uncomfortable as can be imagined. I had to smile later when we were back at sea at her antics in 'softening up' these garments including tying them tightly on a line and dragging them for hours behind DJV. The amount of dye that came out could have re-coloured our mainsail (if I had been happy with purple or orange).

Our last half day was spent processing paperwork to get out of India. It felt like our time in Cochin had gone very fast.

Very early in our journey, before we left Malaysia, knowing we were behind the fleet, I discussed the options with Beverly of making brief stops at Cochin and the Maldives, rather than bypassing both and going direct from Sri Lanka to Salalah, Oman. We had agreed that a brief look was better than none at all, although it would mean an extra 300 nmiles sailing. However, after five busy days in Cochin, during which time we seemed *not* to have seen anything of India, I wasn't so sure this decision was the right one.

But right decision or not, 07:15 on the 20th February we were out of Cochin never to return, unless I win a 1st Class air ticket in a raffle.

Chapter 5

COCHIN, INDIA TO THE MALDIVE ISLANDS ... FROM 20TH TO 23RD FEBRUARY 2010

It would be fair to say we were glad to leave Cochin behind, primarily due to the bad experience we had with our druggy agent. We could have given him the push and found another agent but we just didn't have the time to mess around. Plus, we hadn't seen anything of India, the whole purpose of our brief stay.

The 269 nmile journey to the Maldives was, in the main, boring and uneventful. DJV was fighting a strong northerly current and winds were light, meaning we had to fire-up one engine for most of the first two days. Distance covered 24 hours out from Cochin was a painfully slow 89 nmiles, an average of 3.7 knots; not so good. Ditto for the second day when we covered just 93 nmiles at an average of 3.9 knots.

Shipping was light but that didn't mean we could relax. Noon on the third day found us with a 10 knot NW'er, which felt like a cyclone after the doldrums we had suffered the previous two days and Beverly revealed her *'sail-setting'* expertise in the new breeze.

Late afternoon we had a large container ship attempt to run us down and we did a 360° turn to avoid it. What are these guys thinking?

- Is there anyone on the bridge?
- Is their radar working?
- Are they using us for sport? Are they bored stiff and saying to each other *"so let's run this yacht down to brighten our day"*?

The only positive thing about the incident was it broke *our* boredom and gave us something to do. It was proof, however, that you have to be on lookout all the time.

DJV anchored off the island of Uligamu, Maldives at 08:15, on the 23rd February 2010 … and it was beautiful.

- We had travelled 269 nmiles in 73 hours
- An average speed of 3.7 knots. Our slowest leg yet.

ULIGAMU ISLAND, MALDIVES, 23rd to 25th FEBRUARY 2010
Lat: 07°04'68N, Long: 072°55'34E

Uligamu Island authorities are quick to answer your VHF channel 16 radio call ashore; in fact I thought we were being invaded by the crew in the speed boat which came to DJV with the harbour-master, navy and army personnel aboard. *Scary!* But it was fine and they accepted Bev's hospitality of a cold coke

Beautiful colours of Uligamu Harbour.

(emptied the 'fridge in fact, as there were seven of them) and we settled down to business without delay. No hand-outs or bribes required here (what a breath of fresh air).

We were then allowed ashore to be *'briefed'* by the agent handling visiting yachts. He was a pleasant young man who took his job very seriously. It took him 45 minutes to relate a story regarding another visiting yacht which 'broke-the-visa-rules' by over-staying their visa and then, after being towed into the capital Male (as their yacht had been impounded) broke their confinement and did-a-scarper late one night ... costing his company US$10,000.00, as they were responsible for the yacht's visa.

> *Once anchored at Uligamu Island you are not permitted to raise anchor to visit any other islands of the Maldives Group... unless you pay a fee of US$750.00. Wow and hells-bells!*

The Maldives authorities have a very queer ruling regarding visiting yachts. Once anchored at Uligamu Island *you are not permitted to raise anchor to visit any other islands of the Maldives Group unless you pay a fee of US$750.00. Wow and hells-bells!* Obviously these people didn't want yachties spending money in the Maldives! Our visa allowed us to stay at anchor but not to move until we were ready to leave. So, we saw nothing apart from Uligamu Island. (There was a power boat service from Uligamu Island to a nearby island, but its infrequent schedule didn't fit in with the period of our stay.)

Upper - Kids from cruising yachts ... Lucas and Nina practicing their School lessons.
Centre - On-board Concert performed by (L-R) Kara-Lucas-Nina.
Lower - Main Street of town on Uligamu. Beverly with Agents.

In going ashore on Uligamu, one can't help being impressed by the beauty of the island and its white coral sand beaches and crystal clear water. *(It reminded me immediately of Hills Inlet on Whitsunday Island off the central Queensland coast of Australia, arguably the most beautiful area on the Great Barrier Reef.)* There are no paved streets in the town, just pure white coral sand, no vehicles that we saw and few motor bikes. The agent was quick to supply us with water and petrol/benzene at a reasonable price and there was a very small store which Beverly sniffed around. Do not rely on stocking up with food stuffs here.

There were two other yachts at anchor near the entrance to the harbour and we made new friends - Werner, Lucia, Nina (eleven years old) and Lucas (seven years old) on 'SV Kleiner Bar' … and Uwe, Ann and Kara (6 years old) on 'SV Magnum'. We ate with them all a couple of times and thoroughly enjoyed a 'concert' the three kids had produced and performed together. And Beverly snorkelled with Lucia around the coral reefs near the yachts. It was bloody hot!

I don't know how long the 'Magnum' and 'Kleiner Bar' families had known each other, but it's very common for yachts with children living on-board to be travelling in company, sometimes in quite large flotillas. The *big* problem parents have of course is to keep the kids busy and diverted from the boredom of long cruising legs. All kids seem to have correspondence schooling programmes to work on, with one or both of the parents taking on the role of teacher. In the case of these two particular yachts, they would meet regularly (seldom travelling side by side as their cruising speeds were different) but with prearranged meetings at a certain latitude/longitudes when the kids would swap yachts and have a sleep-over on the other yacht. In the dead-calm conditions across the Arabian Sea they also made the best of this swap-over time to have a swim.

Chapter 6

THE MALDIVE ISLANDS to SALALAH, OMAN ... FROM 26TH FEBRUARY 2010
Lat: 16° 56'14N, Long: 054°oo'39E (Salalah)

On leaving the Maldives at 07:00 on the 26th February 2010, we were looking at a very long journey to Salalah, Oman - roughly 1300 nmiles taking around 2 weeks. A few curious souls have asked me how I *mentally* prepared for such a long journey, out of sight of land for so long. And in considering this question I must admit I had no special formula. I think the answer lies in my mental attitude of not accepting the possibility of breakdown and failure. I just adopt a very positive attitude and try not to let negativity creep into my thinking at all. Though in saying that, there have been five times in the past when I have been seriously scared and ended up *talking to the God Poseidon.* In descending order of scariness, they are:

- The night DJV was anchored at Lumut,

Because of the risk of pirates, big ships are known to run closer to the coastline of Oman without lights ...

Malaysia, at night, when a 60 metre steel barge hit it.
- South of Coffs Harbour, Queensland, in stormy conditions, when DJV reached 14.3 knots, buried her port bow down about four metres and spun around 180°.
- Surfing down a huge swell coming into Jervis Bay, New South Wales, Australia when DJV reached 17.3 knots.
- At night in the Brunei oil fields when I drove DJV into an unlit, steel ship mooring buoy twice within a week.
- The tidal wave out from Aceh, Indonesia must crack a mention here.

I knew I had to maintain my usual positive attitude for our entire journey of over five months. That's a long time at sea, travelling through '*risky*' territories with weather always an unknown.

From the Maldives onwards, one starts to get a feel for the **threat of piracy.** At Uligamu Island, people had asked us about our preparations for such an eventuality. I worried a bit about these questioners as how do we know they aren't a forward guard for the pirates? On the other hand, maybe I'd been watching too many movies which had made me a bit paranoid?

Because of the risk of pirates, big ships are known to run closer to the coastline of Oman *without* any lights, so watch-taking must

> *... a cry went up from Bev; "LLoooooyyyyd, the chart-plotter's crashed".*

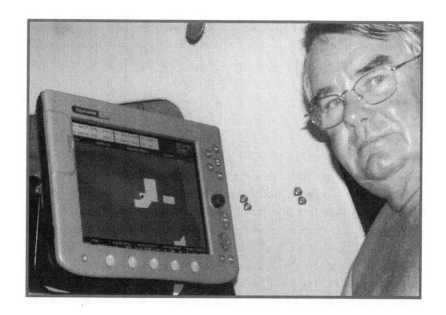

Upper - Chart Plotter which 'crashed' half way across the Arabian Sea
Lower left - Time for a much-worn Aussie flag to be retired-to-the-deep.
Lower right - Beverly became an expert with 'Sailmail' email system.

be taken even more seriously. Radar is a great asset. One hears a great deal of radio chatter on Channel 16 from Coalition Warships patrolling the Arabian Sea and the Gulf of Aden. There are a lot of them and they clearly take their responsibilities very seriously.

Bev and I had awoken on the 26th February to a dead-calm sea and we had to fire up the 'steel spinnaker' to get us away from the Maldives. We motored all day until at 18:00 a ten knot westerly blew up, giving the Yamaha a short respite. It didn't last long though and at midnight we were relying on the motor again. I couldn't work out the currents in this area, as we seemed to be heading into a strong current from the north. The first 24 hours out from the Maldives found we had only travelled 89 nmiles at an average of 3.7 knots. Very ordinary.

At 15.00 on the 28th February, a cry went up from Bev; *"Llooooyyyyd, the chart-plotter's crashed"*. Checking, this was indeed the case, we then talked options. Such an electronic failure has the potential for producing a disastrous situation. No chart-plotter meant we had no way of knowing in which direction we should be travelling. It also meant the chart-plotter had lost its ability to 'talk-to-the-auto-pilot' and keep us on course. All of this might mean we could be manually

Through the 3rd, 4th, 5th and 6th days we continued motoring 24 hours a day and the hum of the engines started to drive us mental. "Holy Cow Batman", was Beverly's curse!

steering for the next 12 days! I suggested to Bev that we could be tricked into motoring around in circles until the fuel ran out? *(I was only joking; what a mean bastard I am!)*

In the early minutes of the crash, we had talked about an additional option of returning to Cochin, India, for repairs and I had been relieved to hear that Bev had a very positive attitude toward the idea of carrying on. I had had an electronic charting system (MaxSea) installed on both my computers back in Langkawi, Malaysia. These installations were for just such a situation as this in that they would provide a backup to the 'Raymarine Navionics' system in the C120 Raymarine Chart Plotter. And loading the newer Acer computer as well was a backup to the first computer failing. Goodness, I'm a careful sod. So, up came my old computer and it took no time to fire it up and have *'MaxSea'* show us the way. The 'MaxSea' system relies entirely on a small, round 'button GPS' (about 50 mm in diameter) attached to the computer. What an incredible little unit it is in its capacity to send a microwave signal to 8-10 satellites overhead and get a precise reading of DJV's position. Then, MaxSea via the GPS system would give us a reading towards our destination - Salalah, Oman. I'm always amazed at this technology. The auto-pilot is a separate system from the chart-plotter, though when they are connected by solid wiring, they work in tandem. Our new found MaxSea system wasn't able to do this, as we didn't have a solid wire connection. It can be done though by manually tuning to the course given us by MaxSea for the auto-pilot to steer by. If

DJV wandered off-course, we could correct it with the press of a button. The auto-pilot will still work on 'Wind Vane' mode as well. This is a setting whereby the skipper can select an angle to the wind to sail by and the auto-pilot will maintain that angle/setting even when there's a wind shift. It can save a lot of sail-flapping and loss of time through stalling sails.

Our 3rd day out found us just 92 nmiles further along our passage. This was going to be a loooooong journey - 1063 nmiles still to go. At 18:00 on the 1st March, 2010 the wind had returned and we had caught the westerly current. By midnight the wind had gone again. *Bugger!*

Beverly reported a large ship passing close-by and going fast. Fortunately, we weren't seeing many of them as we were well north of the shipping path.

Through the 3rd, 4th, 5th and 6th days we continued motoring 24 hours a day and the hum of the engines started to drive us mental. *"Holy Cow Batman"*, was Beverly's curse! When changing shifts and retiring to our respective bunks we would stop the engine on the side of the person off-duty which made for a much quieter rest period and this routine also kept the work-load for the engines equal. The winds had been so slack for so long we had ended up motoring for six and a half days non-stop. It could be said we were suffering from the Doldrums! It wasn't until 08:00, on the 6th March, that an 8 knot breeze developed and we were able to rest the engines. Thank God for the new Yamaha outboards. Many yachts experienced similar wind conditions and quite a few suffered failed mechanical units (gearbox, engine mountings, drive couplings between gearbox and propeller shafts, one

Upper left - SV Kleiner Bar with Lucia, Kara and Werner.
Centre left - DJV on glassy calm seas for over six days.
Centre right - Lloyd chatting to kids on Kleiner Bar
Lower - L-R Lucas, Kara and Nina at their favourite position on the ship.

even had an engine blow-up) and needed repairs due to the seemingly never-ending reliance on engines.

"Ahoy, 'Kleiner Bar' here" ... 15:00, 2nd February 2010

When we left the Maldives we also left SV Kleiner Bar and SV Magnum behind as they planned to spend another day at the Island. Just over four days out from the Maldives, with Kleiner Bar having left a full day behind us they caught us up and boy, was it good to see them. Werner, Lucia, Nina and Lucas were in good spirits despite being well behind SV Magnum. We had seen another yacht pass us to the south that same day and it would have been Magnum but, disappointingly, they hadn't come alongside to say hello.

There was a short swapping of curses about the lack of wind, a flurry of photographing each other (which we later swapped) and they were on their way.

Both the other yachts were obviously motoring a lot faster than us, their 50 horse-power diesels doing the trick. We got our own back on Kleiner Bar though later on when we caught up with them at Port Suwakin, Sudan, due to their yacht having broken a rubber coupling between their gearbox and the propeller shaft. And we were three weeks ahead of them by the time they moved again. So much for 50 hp motors and greater speed!

'ANTI-PIRATE' POSITION REPORTING

A few clever skippers of yachts travelling through to the Red Sea prior to us had devised a very good 'position reporting system' in which yachts sailing in a loose group, via HF radio, could confidentially report their position to the rest of the fleet on a pre-determined radio schedule.

Without giving the system away I will attempt to explain how it worked. The 'Skipper' of the whole scheme had devised a group of waypoints which didn't represent any particular location. They were simply waypoints from which you could pivot a location. One was in the middle of the Saudi Arabian desert, another near India's west coast and a third close to Somalia. Each was given a short name.

To calculate your position and to report on it to the rest of the fleet you would choose any one of the three waypoints (papa or alpha or bravo) and using your chart-plotter (MaxSea) put your curser on, say, 'papa'. This would give you two bits of information: (1) the distance from your boat to papa and (2) the course/compass angle to papa from your vessel. Then to confuse any eaves-dropping pirates, you were instructed to complicate the data by adding a formula to the readings. A report would thus be totally senseless to anyone not knowing the makeup of the formula.

It would be inappropriate to explain this in any more detail as its still being used today. Sufficient to say Kleiner Bar, Magnum and DJV knew exactly where each other were each day and were confident anyone picking up our conversation would not have a clue. *A very clever system.*

With keeping the VHF (short range) radio on Channel 16 at all times we were constantly bombarded with radio messages from coalition warships patrolling the area for pirates. There are a surprising number of nations represented in this endeavour: USA, UK, Japan, India, Iran, Malaysia, Oman, Djibouti and Australia and others and it's very comforting to know they are there. They had a standard chatter which included the latitude and longitude of the vessel they were trying to communicate with. Often that vessel wouldn't reply, sometimes, maybe, because its radio strength didn't anywhere near match the wave strength of the warship and therefore wouldn't be picking up the radio message. Another reason could simply be ... they didn't have their radios turned on.

At noon on the 7th day, (4th March 2010) an 8 knot breeze sprang up from the north and strengthened to 15 knots (NNE) at midnight then slackened back to 2 knots by 06:00 the next morning.

On the 8th day, to break the monotony, we had a visitor in the form of a black and white bird about the size of a seagull. It was unafraid and we guessed very tired. It stayed through the night on the top of the starboard winch and was gone in the morning. Such birds will not accept food or water, seeming to want just one thing ... rest.

9th day, with 555 nmiles to go to Oman, we took Kleiner Bar's lead and stopped all activity to swim in the cool Arabian

On the 10th day our friends from SV Magnum (100nmiles ahead of us) reported two large freighters passing them at night with not a single light showing, not even navigation lights.

Sea, making sure we had mooring lines attached to us from DJV. It would have been a nasty disaster to see the Seawind sailing away, nobody on board! On-again, off-again breezes terrorized us through the 10th day and then, hardly trusting our luck, we nervously enjoyed constant, medium-strength breezes for the 10th, 11th and 12th days.

On the 10th day our friends from SV Magnum (100nmiles ahead of us) reported two large freighters passing them at night with not a single light showing, not even navigation lights. Presumably they were trying to remain as invisible to pirates as possible. But, what a scary scenario these fast moving monsters are; difficult enough to keep tabs on them through the day, now they were motoring at night, completely invisible, apart from on the radar. I did wonder why they considered the pirates would not have detected them with radar.

With our chart-plotter on-the-blink we didn't have the luxury of radar so our night shifts became more nerve-racking.

Toward the end of the 11th day we had been *sailing* for 72 hours, (3 days) non-stop and this was a great relief for us mentally and for the average consumption of fuel. Winds then returned to being 'fluky' and disappointing. We were 240 nmiles from Salalah, Oman.

By now, Bev and I were very tired and looking forward to a week's R&R in Salalah. The winds had collapsed completely again making the final leg into Salalah disappointing due to the calm conditions. In thinking later about the lack of winds along this leg, we imagined the opposite situation and what would it have been like with 40 knot winds and mountainous seas. Really, in retrospect, we considered ourselves very fortunate. DJV arrived at the Port of Salalah, Oman at Noon on the 12th March, 2010. We had travelled;

- 1,396 nmiles in 341 hours (14 days 5 hours)
- Averaging 98 nmiles per day
- Average speed of 4.1 knots.

Not too bad really considering DJV motored for so long. The Yamahas had consumed 260 litres of fuel and between them, ran for a total of 190 hours, an average consumption of 1.37 litres per motor per hour. This meant DJV had motored for more than half the duration of this journey. We arrived with just 15 litres of fuel to spare.

It was great to see other yachts including **Kleiner Bar** and **Magnum**. On entering the modern harbour, we passed several yachts heading out on their way to the Red Sea, the way we would eventually head ourselves after our break in Salalah.

Chapter 7

SALALAH, OMAN ... FROM 12th MARCH, 2010
Lat: 16° 56'14N, Long: 054° 00'39E (Salalah)

Salalah was a sight for sore eyes, we were very weary. Unimaginable how hard this journey would have been in rough weather; we would have lost body weight for sure rather than putting it on as we had.

Salalah Harbour is quite a new port and very modern. As well as a container shipping terminal, it was obvious some of the fleet of coalition warships use it as a supply base. There were six warships in port when we arrived, notably none flying a flag of their country of origin. It looked a very busy port and I guessed a good percentage of consumables for Omani nationals would come through here, hence the strict security.

DJV wandered around the harbour, avoiding huge docking container carriers and tugs and eventually found other yachts at anchor at the furthermost extremity of the port. It wasn't until we were about to drop anchor that the VHF radio crackled into life and we were **told** where we would anchor. The harbourmaster's office was on a steep hill directly above and no vessel moved that he didn't see.

A SAILING ODYSSEY-Malaysia to the Mediterranean

Upper - Warships and Commercial mix it here.
Centre - And at the southern end of the harbour are the ancient fishing boats.
Lower - Then they find a spot for visiting yachts.

This was my first experience of anchoring stern-to-the-shore, hanging off your own anchor and tying to rocks ashore from stern cleats. Doing it this way meant they could fit twice the number of yachts in ... it's just inconvenient to have to use your dinghy to get ashore.

Then came this lion-like bellow, directed at me: *"Déjà vu, here!"*

"What"? I replied, thinking this big, black fellow dressed in a Persil white gown, was the epitome of ignorance. Then I heard a quiet voice from the boat alongside us "Get him while you can; when he disappears only God knows when he'll be back." This lion was our agent, Mohammed and he wanted us ashore, *now*.

"We have just landed and are dying of hunger and thirst; we'll be ashore in 20 minutes." And he waited and then we did the paperwork and crashed for the rest of the day.

I was to learn before I left that this guy was an infamous conman.

- Mohammed had a monopoly and made handsome profits from his empire, thereby allowing him to brag about the BMW he drove. He charged US$100 per vessel, to jump you through the immigration, customs and harbour-master paper-hoops.
- He hired out a small fleet of cars.
- He arranged for fuel, although you paid dearly for it. It was against the rules to go outside the harbour complex to the local service station for

fuel at half the price. But, I learnt later of yachties hiring a car for a day's touring and secreting jugs into the boot then filling them and returning, hoping a search of the vehicle wasn't too thorough.

And you had to help yourself to water from the wash troughs of the men's shower block. Beverly considered this very unhygienic.

Oman was a bit of a blur initially and we were only there five days. **Magnum** and **Kleiner Bar** left after spending just a couple of days resting during which time we shared pleasant meals with them at the 'Oasis Restaurant'. This was probably the only western style restaurant in Oman and was frequented by many ex-pats and all the sailors that came to the Port of Salalah. The first night I enjoyed the last of their large T Bone steaks, with a dead-cold beer. *Just Bliss.*

We were intrigued by vehicles coming in the opposite direction flashing their hazard lights and quickly realised they were warning us of some hazards on the road ahead ... camels.

The next day, Beverly donned her Muslim clothes and we hired a car from the **crook** and drove to the city of Salalah, about 20 kilometres north. The primary task was to post the chart-plotter back to Perth, Western Australia, for repairs. With a lot of effort we found a 'DHL' office (no FedEx) and US$250 later, the parcel

Upper - Bev at fishing village 'Mirbat'
Centre - Inspection of ancient ruins of 'Khor Rawri'.
Lower - Road hazards ... camels.

was on its way. The master plan was to have it delivered back to us in Aden, Yemen but I couldn't help wondering if I would ever see it again.

We also found a would-be western style supermarket (Lulus) which allowed us to replenish some food items. The goods on the shelves were a strange assortment of sweets, chocolates and tinned fruit – non-essentials (maybe that's being harsh, but, to me many such items were 'non-essentials' when to Beverley or other yachties they may have been more essential).

Beverly enjoyed driving our left hand drive vehicle and we travelled north on the modern bitumen two way highway. We were intrigued by vehicles coming in the opposite direction flashing their hazard lights and quickly realised they were warning us of some hazards on the road ahead, **camels** (similar problem to kangaroos in Australia, only much, much larger animals). I would have loved to have seen what remained of a car after hitting one of these monsters. They were a pleasant, slow moving diversion and they ruled the highways. With the rolling sand dunes it seemed we were definitely on the outskirts of the Saudi Arabian desert although this was not literally true.

> Mohammed: *"Do you have the insurance papers for the yacht?"*
> Me: *"No, we don't have insurance."*

We drove about 100 kilometres north and discovered a wonderfully ancient and largely demolished fishing town, 'Mirbat'. Its older sections looked as though it had been used for artillery practice and in fact there was a Battle of Mirbat, which took place on the 19 July 1972. We enjoyed our two hours here immensely. The young boys swimming in the bay soon overcame their shyness and surrounded us asking all sorts of questions. Just a pity we couldn't understand a word they were saying. Typical of young people, they loved having their photos taken and to see themselves afterwards on the small screen.

Large fishing boats were alongside the new wharf and fishermen were working on mountains of heavy netting on deck. I feared ever entangling one of these, as you would be caught but good, for a long time.

We turned our little car south again. Beverly had been told of an ancient port along the coast, halfway back to Salalah port. We had missed it on the trip north. Being more vigilant we found the entrance to the **Port of Khor Rawri,** a spectacular site dating back to around 400AD. This is a world heritage listed site, appearing to have archaeologists still working it.

Once back on DJV we agreed we had water, fuel, food and gas and had enjoyed a five day, reasonable rest to strengthen our minds and bodies. It was time to jump through the customs/immigration and harbour-master rings again, to get out of there. An appointment with Mohammed found us ashore.

Mohammed: "Do you have all your papers and some US dollars?"

Me: "Yes of course."

Mohammed: "Do you have the insurance papers for the yacht?"

Me: "No, we don't have insurance."

Mohammed screwed up his face in a well-rehearsed grimace and said: "You must have insurance otherwise the harbour-master will impose a US$150.00 fine."

Me: "*Bullshit*, it's my decision whether I have insurance or not."

Mohammed had been through this argument many times before; in fact he'd given up arguing and just said, "We must talk to the harbour-master."

And we obediently drove up the hill to the harbour-master's office. Once there, it didn't matter what I said or did (including me being uncharacteristically noisy) he wanted his US$150.00.

"And surely you must have heard of the Muslim practice of women covering their bodies, so as not to embarrass us." Pointing at Beverly he continued, "I would appreciate it if she would leave my office immediately." Beverly, in her rush to get out of Salalah and not realizing we would be visiting the Harbour-master had been wearing her comfortable but *short* shorts and had become a target for this king rat's criticism. Beverly left, in tears.

I had no choice but to part with the US$150.00 with the alternative being to stay in Salalah forever! We learnt later that some forewarned yachties would forge insurance papers which would apparently be readily accepted.

Toward the end of our stay fifteen yachts arrived from the west, the Vasco da Gama Yacht Rally. (This was an organised rally making its way down the Red Sea from the Mediterranean and across to India/ Malaysia, the opposite direction to our journey.) It broke our hearts to realise Mohammed was going to make US$1500 in fees from their visit. Our memories of Salalah, Oman were dented enormously by the dealings we had with this agent and his sly boss-on-the-hill.

Chapter 8

SALALAH, OMAN to AL MUKALLA, YEMEN ... FROM 17th MARCH, 2010
Lat: 14° 31'25N, Long: 049° 08'89E (Al Mukalla)

We left Salalah in dead-calm conditions: nothing had changed weather-wise since our arrival. And the prediction from the crews of the 'Vasco da Gama Rally' was correct; we headed straight into a ¾ to 1½ knot current from the west. On with both motors, breaking my policy of only ever running a single motor; without this change of heart we would, almost, have been going backwards. It was so calm and cloudless and at night we enjoyed a wonderful mirrored, eerie effect of the stars reflected on the flat sea.

To make ourselves a little more 'arms-length' from pirates, advice (which we stuck to) had been to sail no closer to the coast than 10-12 nmiles. Why only 10-12 nmiles? In 1980 the US Navy established twin channels down the centre of the Gulf of Aden, known as the Maritime Security Patrol Area (MSPA), hoping they could concentrate their 'minding' efforts on these channels, but it didn't work long-term. Hence the newer ruling; 'not to sail closer than 10-12 nmiles from the Yemen coastline'. Our friends on *'SV Kleiner*

Bar' and ***'Magnum'*** were two days ahead and reported they experienced calm and no pirates all the way to Aden. They had decided not to stop at Al Mukalla, Yemen.

Three days away from Salalah, Oman, heading toward Al Mukalla, DJV was averaging a slow 87 nmiles per day. The head current was hurting and had increased to 2 knots. I can hear a reader asking, **"How do you know Lloyd, your water speed paddle was disabled, remember".** Correct observation but I had dreamt up a way to calculate current strength and it seemed to work.

- Take note of the SOG reading (speed over ground) into the current.
- Turn DJV 180° and take another reading. It's not convenient to do this under sail but when just motoring, it's easy.
- If we had been running into 2 knot current, our SOG should now increase by 2 knots. **Got it?**

We noticed one of the mainsail saddles (a fabric strap which is sewn to the mainsail and then threaded through the batten cars, nine of which attach the mainsail to the mast) had come adrift and I'm sure Beverly gave a great sigh of relief as she now had something *manual* to do. Perched on the cabin roof in the sun, needle and thread in hand, calm sea; how can it get any better than this?

On the fourth day from Salalah, at 07:00, we entered the harbour of Al Mukalla, Yemen, and enjoyed another 'gunship' welcoming committee like we'd had in Galle, Sri Lanka.

Upper - Beverly repairing mainsail saddle.
Centre - Welcoming gunboat at Al Mukalla harbour.
Lower - They were fishing boats ... we think?

- Distance from Salalah, Oman: 348 nmiles;
- Time taken: 90 hours (3 days 18 hours);
- Average speed: 3.86 nmiles per hour;
- Engine hours run: port, 84, starboard, 86 hours.

AL MUKALLA, YEMEN, HARBOUR AND SURROUNDS ... 21ST MARCH 2010

Al Mukalla is 260 nmiles east of Aden and is the most important port in the Governorate of Hadramaut (the largest governorate in South Arabia). Following the gunboat, DJV entered the harbour to berth alongside the wharf only to see thousands of goats being herded along the same wharf - imports from Somalia.

We needed an agent again, and were blessed with a young English speaking Yemeni chap. He steered us through the immigration/customs/harbour-master hoops (all done by the same man) and in no time we had a clearance card for the main gate. We noticed that the agent slept in his office. To do business we had to wait for him to clear his sleeping mattress and sheets into a storeroom while we stood there watching. No modesty here.

Beverly and I liked Al Mukalla as it didn't have the 'we're-going-to-strip-all-your-money-off-you' attitude found in Oman.

The Harbour-master was our first introduction to the local drug *khat*, a small fresh green leaf which according to Google "contains the alkaloid called cathineone, an amphetamine-like stimulant which is said to cause excitement, loss of appetite, and euphoria". Khat is a slow-growing shrub or tree that grows to between 1.5 metres and 20 metres tall, depending on region and rainfall, with evergreen leaves. Many men (and some women) in Yemen use khat, chewing and sucking it. They don't spit out the old chewed leaf, just roll it up into one of their cheeks and consequently, at the end of the day they have a wad of chewed leaf in their mouth the size of a tennis ball. **Wow!**

Our agent found us fuel (we had consumed 140 litres from Salalah, a solid indication of increased fuel consumption when running two engines) but required little else.

Beverly and I liked Al Mukalla as it didn't have the 'we're-going-to-strip-all-your-money-off-you' attitude found in Oman. And the young agent certainly didn't drive a BMW, but, instead a beat-up Jeep Cherokee in which he refreshingly offered to take us on a tour of the surrounding countryside and the City (for which he refused to accept payment). I went into shock for a while.

With Beverly again dressed in her **'do-not-upset-the-locals'** gown and head scarf, we took our tour, feeling very honoured by our agent's generosity. We drove east along the coast where many luxurious houses, overlooking the Gulf of Aden, had swimming pools, most without water in them. Our tour then took us into an area of a significant housing development, situated on a high ridge above the City of Al Mukalla and overlooking the harbour. I was keen to take photos from here as it was a very good vantage point looking down onto DJV.

We ended our tour with a drive through the city of Al Mukalla and a brief stop for bread. It was just after sunset and Bev and I were accosted by many women carrying tiny, snotty-nosed babies. Our agent explained that Al Mukalla is a port for the importation of goats from Somalia and these single mothers hide aboard the ships and enter Yemen, illegally. They have formed a shanty town on the outskirts of the city and I can guarantee there are no 'single mother' benefits here. Maybe a begging existence here is better than an even poorer life in Somalia?

Beverly had been very upset by the mothers and babies, being soft-hearted about people in distress and had retreated to the Cherokee. She had a history with people in need, in Sri Lanka. Bev and her husband and son had holidayed twice at a house which provided staff to look after their needs and became very friendly with them. Sometime after their second visit to Sri Lanka, the western and southern shores were destroyed by the 2004 tsunami leading to a high death toll and huge damage to property. To help, Bev and her husband bought a new TukTuk (a three wheel scooter often used as a taxi which usually carry two passengers) for the house boy at the house they had leased which would give him a guaranteed income for as long as the TukTuk held together. *An extremely generous gesture.*

We noticed an amusing sign outside a Bank; 'It's prohibited for you to bring your AK47 into the Bank.' The sign even had a photograph of the rifle.

Upper - Al Mukalla harbour.
Lower - Al Mukalla Bank sign re AK-47 machine gun.

The following day we walked into the city and the local people seemed quite friendly, almost seeming not to notice our presence ... unless you pointed a camera in their direction. They seriously disapproved of this action. Beverly was again wrapped in her 'Muslim-blending-in' gear and looked very attractive to my way of thinking despite being almost fully covered. She baulked at covering her mouth and nose, but not doing so seemed to be acceptable. I don't have a clue what the local residents thought of her and whether, or not, she was being unnecessarily scrupulous. The local woman, dressed in black, must have been baking as the sun was fierce. Here in Al Mukalla there were many women dressed in black burqa's, doing their shopping, and a very different situation to Salalah, Oman, where the city streets were empty of woman pedestrians all together.

We noticed an amusing sign outside a Bank; *'It's prohibited for you to bring your AK47 into the Bank.'* The sign even had a photograph of the rifle.

Bev and I tried a real 'Al Mukalla coffee'; it was thick, dark and strong and we agreed it wouldn't be a great threat to the 'Starbucks' coffee chain, of which Bev is a serious customer.

At 22:00 hours on the first night, we were awakened by shouts from alongside DJV and hammering on the hull. The harbour-master wanted to move us to make way for an incoming freighter. Using a great number of gesticulations, we gathered he wanted us to follow his dinghy. This we did (not likely we were going to argue) and we were attached to a **huge** three metre diameter, circular steel mooring buoy.

This was going to be some sort of night as DJV wasn't likely to just hang back from the mooring and behave herself. She would yaw and move around restlessly and someone would have to keep watch and fend off when required. And I was so lucky I had a competent, enthusiastic 1st mate on-board to attend to the buoy as Beverly did, fending off most of the night. Around 04:00 she picked up someone shouting from the shoreline asking us to move as we were blocking the channel of a tug wanting to leave. We had been attached to this shitty, seagull-splattered buoy, by one of the harbour crew and he had tied us securely. It was Bev's turn to experience what it was like to climb from the bow of DJV, onto the buoy and untie us. She was a champion and my only regret is I didn't take photos of her during this exploit.

The tug chugged by leaving us to find water shallow enough to anchor. It wasn't too hard once we had allowed for how we would swing amongst the many large, wooden fishing boats anchored in the same small square of water.

DJV stayed in Al Mukalla just two days and we enjoyed it immensely but, it was time to leave for Aden, nearly 300 nmiles to the West.

Chapter 9

AL MUKALLA to ADEN, YEMEN ... FROM 23ᴿᴰ MARCH, 2010

No drama clearing Al Mukalla harbour; we even enjoyed a wave from the crew of the 'gunboat'. Again we found benign conditions requiring the running of two motors despite a two knot westerly-setting current helping us along. This current seems to come up from the south, past Somalia and then split around Al Mukalla, half turning west and half east? We were now heading west with the westerly-setting current, but, no wind!

Even after all the distance we had travelled, Beverly still had trouble settling and resting during her off-duty time. The simple fact was if she didn't rest during her off-shift she would find her weariness accumulating and this could produce a serious situation on watch. I suggested we resort to a new watch schedule of two hours on, two hours off which seemed to improve her sleeping pattern, although I couldn't work out how over such a short period of time.

"This Is Coalition Warship Number 56: Identify Yourself."

At midnight we passed a huge, eye-catching gas flame onshore, indicating an oil refinery. Our first 24 hours found us 129 nmiles from Al Mukalla; pretty good and we were grateful for the help from the current carrying us along.

In the morning, we were surprised (having assumed there were few fish in the area) to sight a small pod of whales and around twelve fishing boats within a two mile radius of DJV. We had been warned that amongst such groups there were likely to be more than fishermen; not pirates, just thieves who would be armed, board your vessel, and steal anything they liked. (A pirate's intention in contrast, is to take the crew for ransom and leave the vessel drifting.) A bit scary really!

Our second day out found us another 112 nmiles nearer Aden with only 52 nmiles to go. We were receiving a lot of coalition warship chatter on Channel 16 and the waypoints they were calling indicated they were only 60 nmiles from DJV. It was comforting to hear them so close. Ten hours east of Aden we picked up a radio call from *Coalition Warship Number 56*. It was calling "a sailing vessel at Lat: 12°46'E, Long: 045°10'E" … and it called a second time. I said to Beverly "Who could that be, we pretty well know all the yachts sailing this area"! At last, the penny dropped and on checking our position I realized *they were calling us!*

US Captain … "This Is Coalition Warship Number 56: Identify Yourself."

We could tell by the latitude and longitude they gave that they were definitely talking to us but, puzzlingly, there was no warship in sight, they must be somewhere well over the horizon. They were lucky to find us listening

Upper - Beverly spotting Coalition Warship 56
Centre - Coalition Warship 56 ... a very large US Navy Cruiser.
Lower left - Fishermen to be worried about!
Lower right: Warship helicopter checking the fishermen.

to the radio (or were we the lucky ones?) as the *'Russian?'* jabber on VHF, between passing freighters, would drive us mad at times and we would often turn the radio off.

I identified DJV to my contact describing the number of crew, our vessel name and so on and explained our intention of sailing to Aden. My contact was very definitely a Yank and soon he said to me -

US Captain ... "You're an Aussie?"

Me ..."Yeah, absolutely mate ... born in Western Australia, a Sand Groper!" (Exaggerating my Aussie slang and drawl). The Officer of the warship wouldn't have had a clue what I was talking about.

US Captain ... "We have Aussie sailors on-board, hang on I'll get one."

About the last thing I wanted to do was talk to an Aussie sailor. Thirty seconds later I was talking to one of the two sailors from the Royal Australian Navy seconded to this US Warship for reasons they weren't likely to disclose to me. We had a great chat being rude about the Yanks in the process, for example -

Me ... "How do you get to communicate with the Yanks, not knowing most of their language and then there's the drawl problem to contend with?"... I could hear the Yanks laughing in the background so I knew the sailor and I were on safe ground. After a good chat, the US radio operator (maybe the Captain?) came back on.

US Captain ... "You're obviously travelling alone - a very bad idea in these waters."

Me ... "Sorry Captain but *Ignorance is bliss.*" And the moment I said those three words I was sorry as I must have sounded very blasé to him. I apologised and we went on with our chat.

An hour later we heard the unmistakable 'chop-chop-chop' of a helicopter gunship, our friends from the warship.

Me … "Captain, I imagine you and your crew are months at sea and lacking some things which come naturally ashore?"

US Captain … "Yaaaah, you could say that."

Me … "Well I have a treat for you but I'm wondering how close you'll come to us?"

US Captain … "Can't say."

Me … "I'm asking my gorgeous 1st mate Beverly, one of the best looking Canadian females you're ever likely to see in these waters, who's in her black and white bikinis, to stand on the port bow of DJV and give you and your sailors a wave. Do you get my meaning?"

US Captain … "Yaaah, sure do. And don't worry about whether we'll come close enough to see her, or not, as we haaaave the stroooongest binoculars and cameras in the woooorld."

Coalition warship number 56 came rocketing over the horizon and passed within a mile of us (that's close) and Bev was there on the bow as promised. It was a good opportunity for me to give a vote of thanks to the crew on the warship, on behalf of all yachties who passed this way for the comfort of their company in these waters. **We parted good friends.**

An hour later we heard the unmistakable 'chop-chop-chop' of a helicopter gunship, our friends from the warship. They swooped low over DJV allowing us to wave our greetings and then hovered just 200' over each of the fishing boats around us, warning them as it were, to stay away from DJV. An hour later they repeated their visit and implied warning. Even so, we still had a solitary fishing boat come within 150 metres brandishing an empty petrol can. I suspect one word from us on the VHF radio and they would have been shredded meat. *What a great service from the US Warship. We will never forget it.*

Our remaining hours 'til we reached Aden were relatively uneventful with a cheery welcome from the talkative harbour-master's radio operator on arrival. In the dark, Aden hides a lot of its blemishes and is a difficult port to navigate. The harbour-master knew this and had an unlit 'gunboat' escort us to an anchorage.

Vital Statistics for the Al Mukalla to Aden journey:

- Distance travelled: 288 nmiles.
- Duration of journey: 61 hours
- Average speed: 4.7 knots
- Fuel consumed: 220 litres
- Engines runtime:
    Port: 56 hours,
    Starboard: 58 hours
- Average consumption per engine: 1.14 litres per hour.

Chapter 10

ADEN, YEMEN ... FROM 25th MARCH, 2010
Lat: 12°47'56N, Long: 044°59'11E (Aden)

We arrived at the entrance to Aden harbour at 22:00 on the 25th March with 25-30 knot winds hammering us from the NE *(where did they come from?).* In the confusion of dealing with a very noisy harbour-master's radio operator and the guiding gun-boat and with DJV going astern ... we only noticed at the last minute a freighter leaving the bottle-neck entrance to the port, from behind a rough stone wall, at great speed and moving past us with about fifteen metres clearance. This is the closest I've ever come to being run down by a large ship! I suppose there was a pilot on-board but**, *bloody hell....*** we were tired and didn't need this excitement!

Aden Harbour is an untidy place, nah, let's not gild the lily, Aden is a rat-hole.

Following the grey-painted gunboat into port on a dark moonless night was a thrill a minute as well. I had Beverly on the bow keeping tabs on its whereabouts and screaming warnings back to me when we were about to run it over. To add to this excitement, there was a large sunken ship on its side, just inside the entrance - a victim of a civil war years before. On anchoring alongside another massive freighter, under repairs, we found ourselves 150 metres from the loudest *disco* in Yemen. It brought back bad memories of the Penang City Marina, Malaysia and its disco located on a man-made island smack in the centre of the marina.

After a sleepless night we moved DJV to a small bay 500 metres away and found ourselves in the company of two other yachts. One was *'SV Farjara'* owned by an Australian couple Neil and Beverly whose paths we would cross a few times on the passage north through the Red Sea (we were to end up towing them when their drive-train failed, just south of the Suez Canal).

ADEN, YEMEN: A RAT-HOLE REALLY

Aden Harbour is an untidy place, *nah*, let's not gild the lily, Aden is a rat-hole. And Aden officials epitomize the saying 'where there's bureaucracy, there's corruption'. Stay away from this place unless it's absolutely vital you have to visit.

The harbour is formed from the remains of an extinct volcano. And entering the city from your vessel, via the only pedestrian terminal, is like being drawn into a spider's web within the volcano, with at least seven spiders, five of them policemen, waiting to devour you. We were unfortunate enough to have two of the biggest descend on us, posing as agents, Mohammed, a non-English speaking weasel and Noas, an English speaking shark.

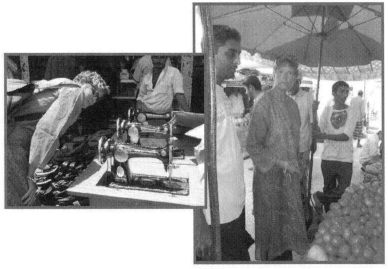

Upper - One of many camel carts at the market
Centre left - Beverly inspecting new 'Made-in-India' sewing machines.
Centre right - Fresh fruit/vegetables market ... with Agents.
Lower - Sunset on Aden.

There's no doubt you need an agent in all these cities, as we did in Al Mukalla and Salalah. In Aden, theoretically, we had a choice, the only difficulty being the only other agent we heard of wasn't on duty when we hit the terminal. Therefore, the 'early bird catches the worm' ... *us!* This couple of bandits had a beat-up, non-air-conditioned car which was to be our coach for the six days of our stay. I said to Bev, "This couple are going to try to eat us alive; let's keep a ledger on how many hours we use their car".

Our first concerns were visiting customs/immigration and the harbour-master. The harbour-master was first and the agents made it easy by taking our passports to the office which was 500 metres from the entry hall. Customs and immigration are situated on the harbour side of the security gate so this meant retracing our footsteps through the Entry Hall, past the Policemen again and walking along the short wharf.

Aden Customs could be written up as a 'sick joke', if the process wasn't so serious. We found the customs chief with his head on the desktop, asleep and, fully spread-eagled on the floor, another person asleep, leaving little room to enter this tiny, centuries-old, accommodation. On being awakened the chief official was quite accommodating and carried out his responsibility without complaint or embarrassment. Immigration was just a bit better; at least they were awake. They took possession of our passports, issuing a 'gate pass' in lieu and I worried about whether we would ever see our small, so important, books again.

FUEL, WATER, FOOD AND OTHER STUFF

Harbour master policy was … if you need dieseline you must buy it from an outlet in the harbour whilst petroleum must be bought from the public service station outside the harbour boundary. We bought petroleum in the company of our agents and our 220 litres cost 65 Yemeni Rial (about US$0.33) per litre which was the cheapest fuel ever offered us to date. It was still necessary to 'grease the palms' of all five policemen to get the fuel past the security gate. One of them even took the lid off one can to sniff the contents to ensure it was petroleum, not dieseline. For those poor souls who don't know the difference between petroleum (benzene in Asia) and dieseline, take the filler cap from your petrol powered car and take a deep sniff. Then go to your neighbour's diesel powered car and do the same. The difference is like comparing the smell of roses to kangaroo dung, with the dieseline comparing to 'dung' in my opinion!!

It was time for re-provisioning and a 15 minute drive across town brought us to a modern mall, situated on the beach overlooking the Gulf of Aden. The mall featured many luxury-item stores, a good coffee house, internet café and a very good supermarket and lots of other services we had no need of. **Hooray and hallelujah!** We spent a good part of the remaining day in this area. It was good to see Beverly dressed in her look-alike-local-clothes as scores of burqa-clad Muslim women frequented the mall and the small, busy town around it. Bev was very comfortable knowing she was attempting to honour the local dress rules.

A WORD ON PROVISIONING MORE GENERALLY

Whilst travelling/cruising the primary commodities required on a regular basis are: fuel, gas, water and food. The greatest disappointment when searching for these goods in Asia or anywhere on our trip was the lack of sophistication in the food services provided. Why haven't Coles and Woolworths invaded these countries? *I know* ... there are too many political, economic, and cultural differences, plus a hundred other reasons. But, I do miss this service when you're forced ashore with hunger only to find few goods from which to choose and at one never to be forgotten place, even strewn on the footpath. (See images of street trading in Al Mukalla, Yemen.)

Singapore is a very modern society and has facilities to rival Australia. Penang Island, Malaysia has a huge supermarket but Langkawi Island is poorly serviced. Patong, Phuket, Thailand had a great supermarket and I used to travel the width and breadth of the island to shop there. But from there through all the countries we eventually travelled, from Malaysia to Turkey, supermarkets were non-existent. The local alternatives were the open markets and many of these supplied almost all you could imagine from sewing machines to rusty car and wagon parts, plus fresh fruit and vegetables, to meat hung in the open (un-refrigerated) and cut to your order. Must admit I never did try that product. (See my write-up on Aden, Yemen and Port Suwakin, Sudan).

Am I complaining? Maybe ... although we did survive through all these areas without any stomach upset! And in any case we always had a heap of baked beans and Vegemite on-board we could have eaten instead. **I wonder *what 'the Canadian'* would have thought of living on them?**

TO QUELL THAT FEELING FOR STEAK!

This was a really strong, busy, Arabic centre, selling everything from mandarins to sewing machines.

That night we asked to be taken to a western-style restaurant which meant another drive back across town to a restaurant near the mall, where the food was very western. We just wanted to taste a real steak again. Can't be sure which animal the steak came from, though it tasted good!

Next day was tour day. Noas and his weasely mate sold us a pre-set tour routine, which we went along with and which turned out to be excellent.

- A visit to a nearby lookout over the harbour and beach
- Another lookout over a bay
- A visit to a small mosque
- Then to a very ancient system of drinking water reservoirs, very ingenious, but no longer in use.
- A long 30 minute drive to the markets which were great ... crowded, colourful and surrounded by camels and their wagons. This was a really strong, busy, Arabic centre, selling everything from mandarins to sewing machines.

Beverly was anxious to have a night away from DJV and booked into the Hotel Mercure, overlooking the Gulf of Aden. This turned out to be an experience she could have done without, given its expense, poor service and lack of *value-for-money*. Bev's fault for leaving the security of DJV!

DJV HOOKED TO THE ADEN HARBOUR FLOOR

We needed water. An arrangement was made with the *'water-man'* at the security gate that we were to bring DJV alongside the wharf at sunset. This we tried to do but found the anchor had snagged something very heavy on the bottom of the harbour, probably another sunken ship?

The harbour is centuries old and you cannot imagine the junk that would be on the bottom. Nearly an hour later, still snagged, I had Bev motor ashore in the dinghy, firstly, to advise the 'water-man' of our predicament and secondly to speak to our agents about getting a diver to dive on the anchor. When she left I made myself a coffee and tried to give my nerves a rest. Coffee finished, I noticed DJV had moved and was in fact drifting. The anchor had fallen off whatever it had snagged and our problem was solved. I therefore steered DJV against the wharf for our appointment with the water-man. *"How many tonnes do you want?"* They sold water here by the tonne. The minimum order was one tonne, so, after filling our tanks, we had water left to give DJV a good wash down.

ADEN CUSTOMS FIASCO ... THE RETURN OF THE 'CHART-PLOTTER' FROM AUSTRALIA ... 31st MARCH 2010

On visiting the Aden 'DHL' International Courier service office, I had been advised the chart-plotter had left Western Australia the day before (27th March 2010) and I was promised delivery on the 30th March 2010. The day arrived and the chart plotter was at 'DHL', but procedurally it had to pass through customs first and the customs office was at the international airport, not far from the markets we had visited a couple of days earlier. Into our non-air-conditioned car and away we went. I had a nasty premonition about this day and attempted to have Beverly stay on DJV or undertake some other activity. I didn't want to risk her killing a Yemeni customs agent (just joking of course, though she does have a short fuse). No, she wanted to come too.

Somehow, the guard at the airport gate became our agent for this procedure and in hindsight I'm certain he was a major player in the subsequent game of extracting-money-from-Lloyd. The *'play'* started and we had five customs people around us in the storeroom and it was becoming very **loud**. These people are great actors and well-rehearsed. Beverly was my immediate worry and I was stern with her, as only

On settling (without Beverly present) with the two taxi bandits (our agents) I had assessed I owed them a bit less than US$100.00 (AU$107.00).

the captain can be and convinced her to sit in the reception area in the cool air-conditioning.

By the time I had the parcel in my hands, 8,000 Yemeni Rial (US$37.00 - not a lot of money, but a lot of hassle) had left my wallet - even the angelic Burqa-clad woman in the storeroom claimed YR2000, it disappearing like quicksilver into her robe. I'm sure the guy from the gate ended up with at least YR2000 and only God knows where the rest went. Two hours later we were ready to leave. **BUT**, the play wasn't over. It was necessary for a customs guard to escort the parcel back to DJV. And then I had to pay for a taxi to get him back to the airport - another YR500.

On settling (without Beverly present) with the two taxi bandits (our agents) I had assessed I owed them a bit less than US$100.00 (AU$107.00). We haggled over the hours they had spent with us and they demanded US$125.00. The Arabs will always haggle for more than they are offered ... *always*. I peeled off US$100.00, shoved it in their hands and walked away, expecting a knife to appear in my back. They said nothing and I just kept walking... they had done alright.

But there was worse to come; the return freight for the chart-plotter had come to 72,135 Yemeni Rial (AU$312) making the total to-and-fro freight cost a whacking AU$534.00. And then came the really disturbing news when I read the accompanying letter from UK Raymarine, the manufacturer. The procedure required to get the unit working again was simply to reboot i.e. reset it -

- Turn the power off to the instrument
- Hold the two lower left grey buttons in.
- Apply power again.

Problem solved and the likely cause of the failure in the first place they said was probably a simple voltage spike. The depth of my negative feeling for UK Raymarine, the manufacturer and the people who wrote the meagre and completely inadequate Owners Service Manual, where there was no mention of a reset procedure, is unprintable. I had more than had enough and said to Beverly, *"let's get out of here"*. And on the 1st April, 2010 we motored from Aden Harbour, never to return.

SUMMARY OF ADEN VISIT ...

- Corruption and drugs are rife here; get used to it. It will be with you until you leave and there's no way around it.
- Keep a record of the number of hours you have the services of the agent (he does, in his own way) as it will be needed when the time of reckoning comes.
- Going through the security gates to your dinghy means passing an average of five policemen (and I use that description loosely) who will all require payment at least once every day. Stick close to your agent at this time.
- **Do not** mail anything to Aden for pickup *(unless it's to save your life)* as Customs will strip you of a

- large chunk of time/money and severely harass you, before you have it in hand.
- Good water is available at the wharf-side and you buy it by the tonne. Anyone who handles the hose will expect an extra payment.
- Dieseline must be bought in bulk whilst in the port, but benzene/petrol from public pumps outside.
- Again, women to be covered.

Happy Days!

CHAPTER 11

ADEN, YEMEN TO PORT MASSAWA, ERITREA ... FROM 1ST APRIL, 2010

From reading about the Red Sea weather, it has a reputation of becoming quite windy from the south when you first turn north into the Red Sea passage from the Gulf of Aden. Our experience out of Aden in contrast, was that winds for the first 24 hours varied from 2 – 12 knots from the SE. Handy but not great! 120 nmiles west from Aden the winds *did* turn south and I was able to dispense with the single engine.

It was around 10:00 on the 2nd April that we had two fishermen come alongside *(where did they come from, I didn't see them approaching?)* and I thought we were in for a rough time *(I must have been getting nervous)*. But they simply wanted drinking water and to show us the huge shark they had just caught. Afterwards, I had a fantasy that this shark had been towing them around the ocean for hours and that's why they'd become thirsty. At least

A cruising yacht, with crew probably feeling a bit weary, anchored off the island recently and promptly received hostile gun fire from ashore.

Upper - Fishermen wanting water and showing us their shark
Centre - A mud-hut village on shore line of Eritrea.
Lower left: A meeting with goat herders on Smyth Island
Lower right - Bev washing DJV after sand storm from Saudi Arabian desert.

they didn't try to sell us anything; they just wanted us to share their excitement. A very pleasant meeting!

We were now converging with a greater number of ships both entering and exiting the Red Sea. They come close together here as the passage pinches in between Yemen on the east and Djibouti to the west. 125 nmiles west of Aden is the turning point into the Red Sea proper! Weenie vessels like DJV have to be very, very careful.

MAYYUN ISLAND, YEMEN ... 2nd April 2010

On this SW corner of Yemen is an island called Mayyun and its only purpose is to accommodate and train Yemeni military personnel. It's like a national park only you are definitely not meant to go near it. Unlike a national park, the inhabitants deal with trespassers pretty sternly. A cruising yacht, with crew probably feeling a bit weary, anchored off the island recently and promptly received hostile gun fire from ashore. They were clearly not welcome, for any reason. *Who needs a pirate threat?*

WHIRLPOOL ENTERING RED SEA ... 2ND APRIL 2010
Lat: 12°38'10N, Long: 043°22'13E

At this point DJV was SW of Mayyun Island and it was around 04:00 and pitch dark. I don't know whose watch it was but we were both on deck. Suddenly Beverly let out a screech *"What's happening to the sails Lloyd"?* All the sails had turned inside out, having been backfilled in a big way! We had steered DJV straight into a tidal-current *whirlpool* and had been turned through the 360° of the compass. The ship that was in front of us was now behind us and then in front again. *Wow!* If you want an unexpected thrill, try this.

I had experienced this sensation twice before, once south of Hamilton Island, in the Whitsunday Island Group, Great Barrier Reef, Queensland, Australia and a second time, again at night, just south of Penang, Malaysia. Nothing you can do about it, because you're turning before you know what's happened and you keep turning. Anyway, after our hearts receded back into our chests, we dropped both engines and powered out of it (relieved that we had not been sucked down into the depths of the Red Sea) a fallacy I think?

We were now officially in the Red Sea and heading north, our destination the Mediterranean (Port Said, Egypt to be exact). From Mayyun Island, Yemen, it was 1273 nmiles as-the-crow-flies and our scheduled first anchorage lay about twenty nmiles ahead.

> *A dust storm came howling across the Red Sea Gulf from Saudi Arabia and we were in for our first experience of the effects of thick dust from an Arabian desert.*

FIRST ANCHORAGE IN RED SEA GULF BEYLUL BAHIR SELATE, ERITREA ... 2nd APRIL 2010
Lat: 13°11'54 N, Long: 042°30'53 E

This was a bay of convenience for us and

there was nothing of interest here, just a little protection from the southerly winds. But we stayed and rested for a day and a night, not going ashore as the water was too rough. This was our first sighting of Africa. 07:00 on the 4th April, 2010 we set sail for Marca Dudo, approximately 60 nmiles north, where, ten hours later we anchored.

MARCA DUDO, ERITREA ... 4TH APRIL 2010
Lat: 13°52'04 N, Long: 041°53'48 E

The Red Sea has twin shipping channels which we had to cross. Shipping channels are lanes marked on navigation charts which guide ships through various risky locations *(check out the charts of the Straits of Malacca, Singapore)*. One lane guides ships north to south and the second guides ships in the opposite direction. Shipping should always pass port to port. The crossing of the twin shipping channels wasn't a problem at all, just a matter of common sense and judgment. As promised, the southerly breezes did spring up on entering the bottom-end of the Red Sea. We were initially sceptical as winds across the Arabian Sea and Gulf of Aden had been almost non-existent, but here we were turning north and what should arrive but a 15 knot southerly. **Hallelujah!** The motors were rested and the crew were smiling again. We dropped the mainsail, 'winged' the jib to starboard and screecher to port and DJV was having a wonderful time.

The first 24 hours out of Aden we travelled a respectable 125 nmiles. And at 17:00 hours on the 2nd April, 2010 anchored at Beylul Bahir Selat'e, Eritrea.

Vital Stats for this run:

- Distance from Aden, Yemen: 167 nmiles
- Moving time: 32 hours
- Average speed: 5.2 knots
- Engine run-time:
  - port: 8 hours,
  - starboard: 9 hours.

DJV was now anchored even closer to the shores of Africa and ashore we could see the *'film set'* of a typical African mud and hessian-built fishing village. What an education to witness first-hand scenes often seen in **National Geographic** magazines. It was a small village just up from the shoreline and I wondered how they arranged for drinking water, the country seemed so dry. In fact it was impossible to take a clear photo of the shore as the air was thick with dust. The local fishermen came close by DJV at times, but never made serious contact. It was a rough anchorage as the winds from the south were building and again, we didn't go ashore because of it.

MARCA DUDO, TO ANFILE BAY, ERITREA ... FROM 6TH APRIL 2010
Lat: 14°45'59 N, Long: 040°47'54 E (Anfile Bay)

The 60 nmiles to Anfile Bay, further north, took ten hours. We had 35 knots blowing right up our back-side and DJV wondered what had hit her. We averaged six knots and anchored in glorious Anfile Bay at 17:00. The Seawind 1000 was in four metres of crystal clear water and it was *hot* so we enjoyed our first swim for a long time. Small fishing sailboats began to sail by, close to us, trying to communicate something by sign-language and pointing out east to the gulf. Oblivious at first, 90 minutes later it was obvious to us what was stirring them up. A dust storm came howling across the Red Sea Gulf from Saudi Arabia and we were in for our first experience of the effects of thick dust from an Arabian desert. We lived with this storm through the night and all the next day and you couldn't see anything further away than 40-50 metres. The dusty stuff found its way into every nook and cranny on board and Beverly was going *mental* as she was the one who liked the boat spik'n'span. "This's just too '*broodle*' (Canadian pronunciation for 'brutal') Lloyd".

Until 11:15 on the next day, we lived with this hot and dusty chaos whereupon I decided we should at least get some mileage out of the wind. 15 minutes later, we pulled anchor and set a course to Port Smyth which would be an overnight trip. We had to trust our chart-plotter to tell us where the shallows were.

PORT SMYTH, ERITREA ... 8TH APRIL 2010
Lat: 15° 32'10 N, Long: 039° 59'53 E

The 80 nmile journey from Anfile Bay was a mixture of weather, with the dust and winds to 20 knots dying away completely by midnight and a two knot

> *Polaroids when sailing are nearly as good as sonar; they can be so effective when looking at shallows but not in the early morning or late afternoon.*

head current requiring a twin motor operation. **Bugger.** I was concerned about running the motors in this region as they do not have air cleaners, so whatever's in the air, such as dust, is sucked into the motors and that's very, very bad for the rate of wear inside the cylinders. But what could you do?

This 20 hour overnight journey found us outside the entrance to Port Smyth at 07:30, but it wasn't a port at all, just a bay with deadly coral shallows at a hard to spot entrance. No buildings and ashore only a couple of goat herders and nothing else. The chartplotter showed a clear, deep entrance and for the first and only time ever, I lost confidence in what the instrument was telling me - a good lesson really, as, based on my experience with this machine, I shouldn't have lost trust in it at all. In 'seeing' only water and no shallow reeves I tried to adopt some logic to the approach to the bay, looking for the two leads into the 'harbour' **(showing on the chart, but in fact not there)** and I ended up bumping DJV across the top of a coral patch. I just kept going, steering away towards where the deep channel was showing and luckily it all turned out OK.

Arriving at an anchorage so early in the day is a trap, as, due to the low angle of the sun to the water, your Polaroid glasses can't pick out the shallows against the deep water. Polaroids when sailing are nearly as good as sonar; they can be *so effective* when looking into shallows ... but not in the early morning or late afternoon.

The only sign of life on this island were two emaciated, but fit, young Eritrean men, the goat herders. Hard to tell their ages, but they looked around 20/25 years old. They seemed to have to fend for themselves having nothing on the island to eat but goat. And I would bet anything they were forbidden to do that.

Beverly gave them water and biscuits.

CHAPTER 12

PORT MASSAWA, ERITREA ... FROM 9TH to 13TH APRIL, 2010
Lat: 15°36'65N, Long: 039°28'27E

DJV was only 40 nmiles from Port Massawa, seemingly the major port of Eritrea. An easy sail until we arrived, at which time it became debatable which entrance to the town we should use, as there were two. There was also a freighter high-and-dry sitting perfectly upright on the shallows off the beach. It had pulled its anchor in a storm, gone aground and never been salvaged. This was a good land mark and I radioed Port Massawa harbour control whereupon a woman answered (very unusual to have a woman working in public life in a Muslim country). I described where we were in relation to the grounded ship and we were directed to the correct harbour entrance.

Port Massawa is a primary port of Eritrea, very old, with an ancient history and it seems half the countries of Asia and Europe have occupied it at some time. And the most beautiful buildings around the harbour, including the impressive old palace of Emperor Haile Selassie, indicate where the invading armed forces have practiced with their artillery over time. There isn't an

A SAILING ODYSSEY-Malaysia to the Mediterranean

Upper - Ship aground and never salvaged.
Centre - Magnificent building after invading forces used it for artillery practice.
Lower left - Water purchased by the tonne ... from the Fire Station bulk carrier.
Lower right - A demonstration of coffee preparation by a local woman.

> *Fish - the open-air market was closed and looked like a cattle slaughter yard. Wow! How do the locals live on this?*

official area for anchoring visiting yachts and we found shallows at the western end of the harbour alongside *'SV Farjara'*, the friends made in Aden harbour.

No agent here so we started wheedling our way through the immigration, customs and harbour-master hoops. Somehow, there are always people who know a few words of English and you are eventually able to sort out who to see and where to find them. This done we set about planning to re-provision DJV. On leaving the harbour, with a 'pass' provided by immigration, we were pounced on by a *local* entrepreneur wanting to make something out of our visit. They are very poor people and you can't blame them for trying to make a 'buck' where they can. We were soon hitched up to a taxi driver and he stuck to us whenever we left the port.

Firstly fuel (benzene not dieseline and you must always be clear about this otherwise you will end up with dieseline every time). At US$1.05 per litre it was the dearest fuel we had to buy on this entire journey to date. Why was it so expensive? Maybe Eritrea didn't have oil reserves, or an oil refinery? Next up were fresh vegetables and fruit. The local market was a disaster so these needs went by the wayside. No such thing as a supermarket and a small deli was the closest we could find. Fish - the open-air market was closed and looked like a cattle slaughter yard. **Wow!** How do the locals live on this? Then our luck changed when the embarrassed taxi driver had the bright idea of taking us to a 'fish freezer works'. Now we were cooking-with-gas. They offered great frozen fillets of cod/groper at a very reasonable price and with a quick calculation on how much freezer space we had, we bought enough to fill the freezer. Drinking water was a bit of a worry. I had to negotiate with the Fire Department and they delivered a tonne to the wharf side out of their bulk tanker. I wondered how good it was and added an extra dob of bleach to kill the baddies. It didn't poison us and even Beverly drank it.

We spent four days here and relaxed-to-the-max including spending time at the coffee shop/bar at the harbour entrance, the proprietor being a friendly chap. We didn't tour inland at all, as I wasn't that keen to leave DJV un-attended.

Time to leave came around quickly. The most exciting time for the crew of DJV came on wanting to leave the Port, well, the country actually. Bev and I fronted up to the lanky, thin, unfriendly immigration officer to gain clearance papers.

Immigration ... "Where are your visas?"

Me ... "In your hands, we just gave them to you."

Immigration ... "No, no, this is only a 48 hour day pass; where is your visa for the other two days?"

Me ... "That's the card you gave us when we arrived, that's all we have."

This chap reminded me of the big thug-man Mohammed of Salalah ... this guy had caught another bunch of cruisers with his sleight-of-hand trick.

Immigration ... "This card is good for only 48 hours, to get away from Port Massawa; you must apply for a visitor's visa."

Bloody hell here we go again around and around and around.

Me ... "Where do we get a visitor's visa?"

With direction received we wound our way from the harbour to the immigration office and two hours later, plus a payment of US$40.00 each we returned to the immigration ***bastard*** to be cleared from Port Massawa. ***And*** an immigration officer had to accompany us back to DJV for him to search the yacht for stowaways.

On pulling the anchor I made two mistakes:

- I failed to radio the harbour-master for permission to leave the port. ***Bloody hell didn't everyone know?***
- I'd turned off the VHF radio, (***the truth is I had never turned it on***) therefore the harbour-master couldn't contact me.

Away we sailed with heightened blood pressure and struggling against the northerly winds, attempting to sail north.

An hour before sunset Beverly says to me, "Lloyd, we have a fishing boat coming up behind us; will you please deal with him." Pounding through a rough sea came

> *This bunch had to be pirates! And just when I thought we had got through Eritrea unscathed.*

> *Much to-ing and fro-ing and the spokesman finally announced they were 'The Eritrean Navy.'*
> *What?*
> *"What's with the gun?"*
> *"Don't worry about the gun."*

this open six metre fibreglass dinghy, taking plenty of spray and all on board looking very wet and uncomfortable. The driver literally 'thumped' alongside DJV as he didn't have great control in these seas. Ahead of him was the spokesman and alongside of him, dressed in army camouflages, was a chap carrying an AK-47 automatic machine gun.

This bunch had to be pirates! And just when I thought we had got through Eritrea unscathed.

Suspected pirate ... "Pull over, stop the ship!"

Me ... "Get lost we're not stopping for anyone."

Much loud to-ing and fro-ing and the spokesman finally announced they were *'The Eritrean Navy.'*

Me ...What? "What's with the gun?"

Suspected pirate ... "Don't worry about the gun."

Me ... "But, I am worried about the gun, I don't like guns."

Suspected pirate ... "I must come aboard to check your papers as you didn't clear Port Massawa correctly."

Around this time I had a short talk to the **God Poseidon** and decided to let this ruffian in worn street clothes, aboard, as **they had the gun** and weren't going away. Bev pulled out our papers, which were all in order. The spokesman wanted to use my VHF radio to call the Port. (After all the hours sailing and tacking, we were still just eleven nmiles from Port Massawa so were within VHF range). He spoke to the woman on the radio in the harbour-master's office, explained all our papers were OK ... and left. And that was that!

Maybe that experience was partly why Bev and I had a *'moment'* the same day we left Port Massawa Harbour. Bev and I had had our 'moments' ... just two and a half that I can recall. Mostly they revolved around Bev's premonition that we were not going to make Turkey in time for her to meet her son at the end of June, 2010, when he would be on summer leave from university. The first pressure valve on this matter *'blew'* coming out of Port Massawa. It was around midnight, Beverly's shift and she came to me with an anxiety that we were not progressing up the Red Sea fast enough! It was the 13th April 2010 and by my reckoning, that meant we still had 10 weeks in which to make this destination, plenty of time in any case I thought. Understanding this point at that moment was lost on Bev, therefore, despite needing the rest I irritably dragged out the computer and printer and wrote and printed a letter describing the reasons for not being able to go any faster. I rounded off the letter by offering to turn back to Port Massawa and to stay with her until she could fly on to Turkey, thereby arriving in plenty of time (10 weeks' worth of time in fact!!!). Bev didn't speak to me for 24 hours, not a single word *(I hate that)* but eventually we came together to discuss the letter. Beverly had misread the letter and in her tired frame of mind had read **"*I was going to 'chuck-her-off' DJV at Port Massawa"*. *WOW***, that must have been a shock for her and with us both then

> *Difnein Island is described in the 'Red Sea Pilot' as an island NOT to be explored because it is littered with land mines. Just lovely.*

sitting down and going through every word of the letter, it was revealed what I had really offered!

The next day all was back to normal between us. Maybe Beverly realised the time still left to us to get to Turkey, did her sums on how many miles per day we would need to average to do this journey in her time frame. As will be seen we held it all together and arrived in Turkey in good time.

DIFNEIN ISLAND, ERITREA ... 14TH APRIL 2010
Lat: 16° 36'37N, Long: 039° 19'74E

From Port Massawa to Difnein Island is 65 nmiles as the crow flies. DJV tacked and scrambled for 119 nmiles, to get there in 31 hours. That equates to two nmiles travelled for every one nmile made towards our destination. I will not try to describe the frustration of sailing/motoring against a 17 knot wind and two knot current. Not that we were sailing towards paradise; Difnein Island is described in the 'Red Sea Pilot' as an island **NOT** to be explored because it is littered with **land mines.** Just lovely mate.

Anchoring in pitch darkness at an unknown island is always a challenge, as we wanted to be on the lee side (don't all yachties prefer the smooth water side?) of the island. But, the water was very deep right up to the short, shallow ledge on the southern leeside coastline. Here, I had to trust in my chart-plotter, depth sounder and radar (how did the olden day sailboats ever manage) to get us close enough, safely, to drop an anchor. With Beverly on the bow waiting to let it go, I kept nudging, nudging, nudging toward the shoals until the gauges started to read we were in shallow water (I like a minimum of four metres, but in a strange country, as we were in now, eight metres would be OK). And the radar was a scare as it showed we were almost on land. Down went the anchor and the crew had a good night's sleep. Next morning revealed DJV was anchored 150 metres from the beach; very good I thought. As for the land mines, we left them alone and come 07:00 carried on to Nawaret Bay, Sudan.

You have to wonder **WHY** any invading/defending force would pick a tiny isolated island such as Difnein to cover with land-mines. There must be a reason but it certainly escaped me!

NAWARET BAY, SUDAN ...16TH APRIL 2010
Lat: 18°14'14N, Long: 038° 19'38E

Difnein Island, Eritrea to Nawarat Bay, Sudan was 130 nmiles as the crow flies which DJV travelled in 34 hours, an average of 3.7 nmiles per hour. I'm not going to claim a speed record, but, I'll bet there have been boats take longer to travel this distance than DJV. Since leaving Port Massawa we had cumulatively run the Yamahas a total of 97 hours. We were pleased to have crossed the Eritrean/Sudanese border. Nawaret Bay was great - no wind, flat water and good protection should the wind spring up from any direction. The calm weather gave us a good opportunity for a Beverly 'photo-shoot' of DJV at anchor. We stayed here 1½ days surrounded by absolute wilderness and it was very peaceful, with the bonus of a small island to explore.

Port Suwakin, Sudan, is one of the smallest ports you will find along the west coast of the Red Sea but the most interesting; <u>a stop-over not to be missed.</u>

Come 07:00 on the 18th April, 2010 we lifted anchor for Port Suwakin, Sudan.

CHAPTER 13

PORT SUWAKIN, SUDAN ... FROM 19TH APRIL, 2010
Lat: 19°06' 42N, Long: 037°20'28E

From Nawarat Bay to Port Suwakin was another 78 nmiles journey that took us 99 nmiles to complete and included a somewhat scary overnight journey because of travelling through thickly grouped coral reef country. The northerly winds were non-relenting and it was *slow* going with both motors working hard again. At one stage we had a school of large fish swimming in company with DJV along with an even larger *shark!* Maybe they were buddies?

Port Suwakin, Sudan, is one of the smallest ports you will find along the west coast of the Red Sea, but the most interesting; *a stop-over not to be missed.* What gives it this unlikely reputation is the fact it continues to reflect such an ancient and traditional Arabic way of life. You step back centuries to times of donkeys, goats and camels, rather than trucks, cars and motorbikes. It has a history dating back to 400AD and the ruins you pass on the way into the anchorage testify to this, thrilling and different, as Bev said, from any other port we had entered. Bev also liked the fact that people wore traditional clothing including some of the tribesmen carrying scimitars *(their traditional curved sword)* and she really appreciated "the culture being visible in the people themselves rather than only being visible by visiting a museum or historical site". Bev also rated the coffee highly, "strong, but good".

There was a *huge* dredger working at the entrance to the harbour and the entrance, to me, despite the chart-plotter, resembled a maze! The ships entering this port were required to berth stern-to, hanging from their own anchor with a drop-down ramp from their stern. I thought that primitive in itself, but changed my mind when I reached Greece and saw how the inter-island ferries berthed.

Port Suwakin is where we caught up with *'SV Kleiner Bar'* as they had suffered mechanical failure from a torn flexible coupling between the gearbox and the propeller shaft. This kept them there more than a month and it eventually put us weeks ahead of them.

Another *big* black fellow in a Persil white gown met us at the shoreline and what should his name be but 'Mohammed'. **Oh no, not another one!** This Mohammed, however, was the opposite of his namesake in Salalah, Oman; he was a gentle giant with a heart of gold and as Bev said he was the best agent we had on the whole trip. Bev and I arrived in Port Suwakin without a cent of local currency and no US dollars. Mohammed was quick to loan us local money until we visited the Port of Sudan about 60 kilometres north, by road.

Upper - Local fishing boat against ancient ruins (Image by SV Kleiner Bar)
Centre - Camel drivers washing camels in the sea water.
Lower left - Beverly and friendly agent 'Mohammed'.
Lower right - Ship backed into small wharf of Port Suwakin.

Suwakin was a fascinating and very photogenic place. It was fun to see camel drivers washing their beasts in the ocean within easy view of us on our yachts. And to see the constant movement of small fishing boats, some with the famous Arabian triangular sails, coming and going from our harbour. I would have loved to have taken some photos of the 'High Security' Army Outpost here as it looked anything but, given that it was just another mud brick building, larger than all around, but with WW1 cannons in the front. My impression of this display of force was that the cannons hadn't been fired in decades; they were just there for display. There were, however, armed guards at the entrance touting rifles although they also looked like discards from WWI. **BUT,** photographs were not allowed and you don't play games with such hosts.

Water was provided to the community via a desalination/water maker and we were sold 400 litres of the best. I have never been sick from poor water, but, I do try to help myself by adding an egg-cup full of washing bleach to the water as it's going into the holding tank.

An interesting aside to life in Port Suwakin, as related by our agent Mohammed, was the fact temperatures here, mid-summer, rise to 60°C; too hot for human existence in his book and mine. All residents move inland 35 miles, to a mountain range, where they have their 'summer' houses and the cool of the mountains allows them to survive. With winter returning, they move back to the ocean.

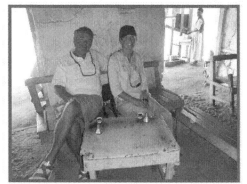

Upper - Main Street of Port Suwakin town site
Centre left - Local coffee shop-no great risk to 'Star Bucks'.
Centre right - Local butcher shop!
Lower - L-R Beverly, Lucas from (Kleiner Bar), Lloyd, Nina.

PORT SUDAN, SUDAN ... 21st April, 2010
Lat: 19°06'42N, Long: 037 °20'28E

We visited the city of Port Sudan by local 20 seater bus - an experience in itself. These buses pickup and drop-off anywhere along the route and we were stunned at where people chose to get off. We would be in the middle of a sandy wilderness and someone would get off and walk into the desert, no civilisation evident anywhere.

Whilst travelling on these buses you have to be very conscious of where you point your camera. Many Muslims have a strong aversion, rooted in their religion, to having their image taken. I nevertheless was tempted to secretly try and take a photograph of a gorgeous big, dark-eyed, four-year-old girl sitting in front of me on the bus and in so doing I felt I came close to the father slitting my throat. Later in the journey I was much more successful taking a portrait of a very handsome, middle-aged woman with ceremonial knife scars across her cheeks.

Having been there, albeit only by bus, our advice would be not to put yourself under a lot of pressure to visit Port Sudan by bus or yacht. Our visit was primarily for money and supplies but neither is it a great town in which to re-provision. Of primary concern is the fact it is a lousy port for visiting yachts. Very rough, stern-to anchoring, much too close to large freighters a short distance across the harbour. We had our suspicions about the charter boat operators at the same anchorage after we had no success trying to recover a knife left with one of them by a yachty friend.

Déjà vu III passing ancient ruins of original town of Port Suwakin.

All good things have to come to an end and we did still have a long way to go to reach the Mediterranean - 735 nmiles as-the-crow-flies, to be exact. So, it was off again leaving Port Suwakin and saying goodbye to *'Kleiner Bar'*. But, not before a 'photo-shoot' on the way out of the inner-harbour with Beverly in the dinghy taking a bunch of images of DJV leaving Port Suwakin, with the ruins of the original city in the background. And they turned out to be great images.

PORT SUWAKIN TO MARSA FIJAB, SUDAN ... 23rd April 2010
Lat: 20°01'98N, Long: 037°11'53E (Fijab)

DJV was struggling to progress northwards even on two motors; a 20 knot northerly wind and a southerly current of two knots seemed to have us standing still at times. Passing through the outskirts of Port Sudan at night was also a real worry with unlit ships at anchor and many unlit steel buoys to contend with.

North of Port Sudan the geography changes dramatically. There's a string of islands running north for 50 nmiles, forming a channel averaging two nmiles wide between the mainland and the islands. And occasionally along this channel you strike human life in the most out-of-the-way-places. On a sandbar at the entrance to Marsa Fijab we discovered a group of twelve local African citizens having a barbecue. The oddest thing about it was the two mini-cars with

Upper - A great shot of DJV in the calm waters of Marsa Fijab, Sudan
Centre - A local group driving/pushing their small car through 500mm salt water.
Lower - A view of DJV from the masthead ... compliments Beverly.

them on the sandbar ... which was surrounded by sea water! We kept a close watch on the group through the afternoon and eventually witnessed them driving/pushing their vehicle through 500mm deep seawater to the mainland! **WOW**, I'd love to inspect these vehicles in six months' time for rusty panels. The underside mechanics of these vehicles (brakes and anything metal) would never be the same again. They apparently had never heard of corrosion from contact with salty water, or they were hire cars?

Marsa Fijab was our first stop after leaving Port Suwakin and a difficult area to enter due to the many shallow sandbars, coral bommies (coral rocks that have grown from the sea floor) and reefs - a true wilderness area. Without the chart-plotter I wouldn't have attempted it (let's face it without the chart-plotter I wouldn't have left Australia). As I've mentioned before, Polaroid sunglasses are also a must, when navigating shallow water.

Bev and I enjoyed this area immensely as it was a perfect anchorage from any weather. For some reason which escapes me now, I hauled Beverley up the mast from where she took great images of the surrounding crystal clear aqua water and sandbars. The next day we took off for Marsar Siyal.

Charging out from the army outpost was a large six metre inflatable, with four tough, fit looking guys on-board.

MARSAR ARAKIYAI, SUDAN (ARMY OUTPOST) ...
25ᵀᴴ April, 2010
Lat: 20° 13' 38N, Long: 037°12'43E

We had been warned about the undesirability of visiting Marsa Arakiyai (en route to Marsar Siyal) a site established as a Sudanese Army outpost the residents of which have a nasty reputation for taking your passport and then holding you to ransom for goods and money. Again, who needs Somali pirates? Therefore, it was never our intention to call in. But the residents must be accustomed to this behavior by passing yachts and have become pro-active. *"Beverly, I think we're going to have visitors, cover yourself kiddo."* Not that Bev wasn't dressed appropriately by Western standards; she just wasn't dressed appropriately by Muslim standards and their stricter code.

Charging out from the army outpost was a large six metre inflatable, with four tough, fit looking guys onboard. They bumped alongside DJV and I made sure I was right there to eyeball them. DJV kept sailing at five knots.

Army thugs ... "We want to inspect your passports?"

Me ... "Get lost; there's no way we're giving any papers to you and we have no intention of visiting your bay." (Language modified for print).

My language was set to tune in with theirs; these boys weren't here to be nice to anyone. I couldn't see any weapons but there were many places they could have been hidden. This abusive verbal intercourse went on for several minutes and suddenly, the penny dropped with them, they were not getting anything from this yacht ... and they powered away for home.

This small mob of soldiers was just that, a mob intent on conning anything from us we were willing/unwilling to part with. Had we shown them our passports I would guarantee they'd have raced back to the outpost forcing us to follow? *"Maybe we're learning and toughening up"* I thought. This meeting had a real scariness element to it, as they outnumbered us in number and strength. Had they produced a weapon we would have done exactly as they wanted.

MARSA SALAK, SUDAN ... 25TH April, 2010
Lat: 20°27'72N, Long: 037°14'16E

This next anchorage was a *puzzle* in as much as it was a wide and shallow bay, but, peppered with thousands of coral bommies. To enter at night would be to ensure disaster and even through the day was a challenge. I would not recommend this anchorage to any sailor.

Here I was to learn of Bev's strong commitment to 'fishing'. We had trolled lures before, but, not too seriously, although my efforts did lead to the loss of two expensive lures. There was a lot of weed floating in the Red Sea and I'm confident the buildup of this scourge led to the overloading of one rig. Or, maybe, we had hooked two fish too large for the gear? Which theory is the most believable? To Beverly, the bottom line was we hadn't brought any fish on-board!

Anyway, on motoring around until we found a clear patch of sandy-bottomed water big enough for us to swing in if confronted by any changing wind, we selected a patch in the lee of a sandbar. This is when Bev spotted fish through the clear water and on my rigging her line, she was kept busy until it was too dark to see. Catch? ***Zero.***

SIYAL ISLAND, SUDAN ... 28ᵀᴴ APRIL 2010
Lat: 22° 47'21N, Long: 036°13'07E

Why I ever chose to go into this area will always remain a mystery to me. Maybe it was shown in the Red Sea Pilot, (which is a manual written by previous clever sailors explaining where the best anchorages are and a million other facts) *"that must be it"*, he said hopefully. But, I would never recommend this anchorage to any sailor trying to navigate the Red Sea. Siyal Island is in a Bay called ***Foul Bay***, so named for good reason - it's littered with millions of bommies. To navigate through the area, I stood on the roof of the cockpit and called directions down to Beverly at the wheel. We were on auto-pilot and I would shout –

"10 degrees to port".
"20 degrees to starboard" and so on.

At one time Bev called back to me, *"We're travelling away from our destination."* And so we had to, to miss the bommies in our way. A very dangerous area. Our company at this anchorage that night included a few fishermen and a boat load of about a dozen soldiers. But they made no contact.

On leaving the island, progress north became equally difficult. At one time I turned DJV 180° to determine the head-on current and measured it at 2.2 knots. We had resorted to short tacking, then longish tacks, then just motoring. It was a struggle. Then, to add to our woes we hooked a large, strong fishing net around the port rudder which swung DJV into a 90° turn off-course. Out with the largest, sharpest knife on board and short work was made of the net now in at least two pieces. Here was a common situation, a long fishing net strung across a passage for vessels such as DJV. My feeling about these incidents is; fishermen set nets in the most unusual and risky areas, always knowing they may be jagged by a ship of some sort. There's a marina on Rebak Island, near Langkawi, Malaysia, where entry is by a dedicated 50-60 metre wide channel. One morning we woke to find a fisherman had anchored a 200 metre net in the centre of the entire length of the channel. Did he not think an outgoing/incoming yacht would trash it? I'm certain he did but risked it anyway!

We had 45 litres of fuel left and it was still 135 nmiles to Port Ghalib; the math's didn't add-up to a successful journey so I made a decision to call at a bay called Port Luli, Egypt, for fuel. **We would have to land in Egypt without a visa - not a recommended practice.**

CHAPTER 14

PORT LULI, EGYPT ... FROM 1ST MAY, 2010
Lat: 24°36'52N, Long: 035°07'05E

DJV had been running both engines for most of the way from Port Suwakin, Sudan (345 nmiles) and although we had taken 80 litres of fuel on there, because of our lack of local currency, I hadn't filled our tanks to the top. This meant on approaching Port Luli, Egypt, our fuel reserves were down to 45 litres, making it obvious we could not make Port Ghalib, Egypt, (117 nmiles north) our next major stopover.

A VHF radio *call-for-help* drew a response from two yachts doing the same journey (one being Alistair and Vivian of SV Largo Star whom we would spend some time with in Italy) and they were only too happy to give us fuel, but they ran diesel engines. It's very rare to find a yacht using exclusively petrol as DJV does. I made an executive decision to call into Port Luli; surely being an Army outpost/town they would have a petroleum/benzene/dieseline station there? And no doubt a Hungry Jacks and KFC? I was however, a little concerned that we didn't have a visa to alight on Egyptian soil.

A SAILING ODYSSEY - Malaysia to the Mediterranean

I have difficulty describing the facilities at Port Luli *(a lovely name);* from the water it seemed there were none. All we could see were a few fishing boats pulled ashore for repairs and two sunken boats which hadn't quite made it and a small mud cubby-house. But then we noticed one solitary person ashore so we loaded four 20 litre cans into the dinghy and away we went.

> *... we communicated our problem and slowly it sunk in that 'we needed benzene' and 80 litres of it.*

The cubby-house turned out to be *the* army outpost manned by two youngish guys, shod in thongs/flip-flops and they weren't that pleased to see us. The only equipment I could see was an old HF radio from the 1st World War and two pups, which were intent on licking us to death. No weapons to be seen, but I'm sure they were there!

FUEL FROM NO-WHERE ...

With red benzene tanks in hand we approached the outpost and we just wore the initially surly, younger soldier down with overwhelming friendliness. We had not a single word in common (he no English, us no Arabic) but somehow, as one must, we communicated our problem and slowly it sunk in that *'we needed benzene'* and 80 litres of it. After getting over that hurdle, it seemed this young man warmed to us (maybe he had taken a shine to Beverly?) as did his older Commander and they also warmed to the idea

Upper - Entering Port Luli's hostile waters.
Centre - No port at all ... just a mud hut and half sunken fishing boats.
Lower - We would call this 'Tiger country' in Australia!

of fixing our problem. Several glasses of hot, sour tea, sweetened with lots of sugar followed. This was not a problem to be rushed.

Out came a mobile phone (the sight of that modern device in the context of the mud-shack surroundings came as a bit of a shock) and the commanding officer connected with a friend somewhere who was obviously in a position to provide the goods. Twenty minutes later, seemingly from no-where, a Good Samaritan pulled into the outpost with 80 litres of the best fuel in two bulk drums. We were asked to discreetly position our cans between the two boats on the beach and the three gentlemen proceeded to decant the bulk fuel into them. It seemed this operation must not be viewed by anyone; we surmised what they were doing was somehow against *all* army protocols.

They would not accept any offers of physical help and even lifted the full cans into our dinghy. I had to smile at this, as the dinghy was high and dry on the beach at the time and I could see what was coming. An attempt was then made to drag the dinghy into the water but of course, *it wouldn't budge.* Eventually the penny dropped and they unloaded the dinghy, dragged it to the water, made sure it was floating, and then reloaded the cans. The cost per litre ... US$0.33. The driver was thrilled with the US$10.00 tip I gave him, but, the army people wouldn't accept a dime. Beverly returned to the outpost with a carton of cigarettes and that went down very well.

An amusing aside to this encounter was the soldiers receiving an incoming radio message and with much gesticulation (mainly patting of the shoulders where epaulets would exist and frequent use of the word *'General'*) we were advised a 'General' was about to visit the Outpost. Off flipped their thongs and out came the army boots to replace them.

We were impressed by this generous friendliness which sadly was not reflected in the behavior of Egyptian people generally during our visit.

CHAPTER 15

PORT GHALIB, EGYPT ... FROM 4ᵀᴴ MAY, 2010
Lat: 25°32'02N, Long: 034°38'32E

Again DJV had to battle 25 knot NW'ers and a strong southerly current so progress from Port Luli was rough and slow. Both engines were still required most of the time as the wind was coming exactly from where we wanted to go and tacking was almost useless due to the strong southerly current. It took 28 hours to travel the 112 nmiles from Port Luli, average speed 3.9 m/p/h. And we were **knackered** when we arrived.

Approaching the entrance to the marina, a 15 metre yacht on its side, high and dry on the beach, didn't create a positive, reassuring impression.

Port Ghalib is a testimony to seemingly unlimited wealth. This great marina/hotel/shopping complex was recently hewn straight into the desert from the Red Sea. It was said a very wealthy Sheik from Kuwait poured an immense amount of money into this project and you couldn't help but wonder **why?** Could it only be because he needed a berth for his fairly modest 25 metre power launch?

Approaching the entrance to the marina, a 16 metre **Beneteau** yacht on its side, high and dry on the beach, didn't help create a positive, reassuring impression. Port Ghalib is a port of entry for Egypt and the officials were efficient enough. The marina policy of berthing boats stern-to the wharf, however, was a fiasco, as the people on the tug-boat and those who came aboard to supervise, were hopelessly inexperienced. If it hadn't been for yachty friends helping from ashore we would have been in deep trouble. At least the marina was modern and comfortable and we were able to catch up with more yachts which had been ahead of us through the Arabian Sea.

It was **not** a great place to re-provision as the shops cater mainly for buyers of luxury clothing and goods. Two kilometres away in a satellite town for the local people are two small grocery stores with a limited range of food etc. I employed a barber here who proved to be a true Egyptian entrepreneur. He just moved seamlessly from a haircut, to a shave, to a facial at which time the 'penny dropped' that this was going to cost me plenty. And relatively speaking, it did; US$10.00. Beverly thought it was a great joke. **She could be so harsh.**

Upper - Welcoming vision to Port Ghalib ... a wrecked yacht.
Centre left - Beverly up-the-mast taking photos of Port Ghalib marina.
Centre right - Layout of marina clearly shown.
Lower left - The few yachts berthing.
Lower right - Berths for any sized power/sailing yacht.

Upper - Port Ghalib was almost all expensive boutique shops.
Centre - I did have time for a haircut, which developed into a shave and facial, how did that happen?
Lower - Lloyd against a fashionable architectural design.

LUXOR BUS TOUR ... 7ᵀᴴ MAY 2010

There was a buzz through the fleet that Port Ghalib was a good place from which to tour the highlights of the city of Luxor, mainly because you could leave your yacht knowing it was well guarded. So Beverly and I booked a tour which included the Valley of the Kings, Luxor Temple, Al-Deir Al Bahari Temple, the Karnak Temple excavations and a boat tour of the Nile River in the vicinity of Luxor.

It was a two day, overnight tour arranged through an agent at the nearby Marina Hotel complex and was very well organised. We were picked up from the marina at an early hour and driven approximately 100 km north to join a foreign tour group travelling for the same reason - a look at the antiquities around Luxor. We found the tour excellent with an expert Egyptologist guide making an impressive presentation of the Karnak Temple on the east side of the Nile and the Valley of the Kings on the western shoreline.

The Valley of the Kings has several tombs located there for various Pharaohs (rulers) who had tunnels and rooms dug into the side of a limestone hill which were then filled with precious treasures. These treasures were to help the deceased Pharaohs travel to their 'final' resting place in comfort and peace. By the time the authorities let mere human being (such as me) into these tombs they have been cleared of all treasures and you are left to investigate an uninspiring 'hole-in-the-hill'! And you were expected to pay extra to walk into Tutankhamen's tomb. What was the point, having been discovered in 1922, it had

A SAILING ODYSSEY-Malaysia to the Mediterranean

Upper - Nile river cruise boat
Centre left - Valley of the Kings country.
Centre right - Typical, romantic Nile river sail boat.
Lower left - This man didn't mind me calling him 'Colonel Gadhafi'.
Lower right - A ketch style Nile sailing boat.

been cleared out decades ago and the contents taken to the Cairo Museum and other museums around the world.

At the Karnak Temple the avenue of the Sphinxes are a monument to the artists who created these hundreds of immense stone lion statues (once stretching for two kilometres) and the 134 huge columns of the Great Hypostyle Hall, most of which dates back 3000 years.

An inspirational 'light show' followed after sunset, over the sacred lake attached to this ancient treasure house, where, centuries ago Pharaohs and their offerings to the gods were purified. Not really sure what this meant but you can assume they were dunked?

After a comfortable night in a Luxor Hotel we regrouped for lunch at a restaurant on the shore of the Nile River, followed by a boat ride on the Nile itself. We were then driven back to Port Ghalib thoroughly tired but very pleased with our two day outing. In having seen these (sometimes seemingly endless) desert displays of ancient Egyptian artifacts I had to decide if I was a real lover of such antiquities; I came up with a ***negative*** answer and decided I would rather keep closer to the ocean and things nautical!

Back to the marina, a complex where we had found there to be a lot of 'love'. The dustman had proclaimed his "love" for me ... and the immigration man had said he had "fallen-in-love" with Beverly. Bev and I agreed that we'll know where to go if ever we feel neglected and unwanted.

Upper - Beverly with 'Lions'.
Lower Left - Lloyd with massive statue.
Lower right - Security was strict!

Before leaving Port Ghalib for our next stop, the excellent Hurghada Marina (111nmiles north), we had filled DJV with 257 litres of fuel (at US$0.85 per litre) taken on water and replenished essential provisions.

CHAPTER 16

HURGHADA, TO PORT SUEZ, EGYPT ... FROM 12TH MAY, 2010

Lat: 27°13'51N, Long: 033°50'50E (Hurghada)

Arriving at Hurghada, we caught up with even more yachts that had been ahead of us, Betty and David of *'MV Sundance'* being the people I knew best having met them on the '2007 Sail Indonesia Rally' out of Darwin, Australia. Another sailing vessel, **SV *Integrity*,** now alongside, was in a very sad state with engine parts strewn all over the galley and other below-deck areas. I had noticed this US yacht at Boat Lagoon, Phuket, Thailand, in 2009, where it had been on-the-hard for almost 12 months having a lot of expensive work done, including an engine overhaul of the six cylinder Ford diesel engine. The engine had started knocking well south in the Red Sea due to one of the big-end bolts having come loose causing one hell-of-a-racket and threatening engine disintegration. Betty and David had towed 'Integrity' all the way from the southern reaches of the Red Sea to Hurghada. 'Sundance' had also towed 'Integrity' in Fiji when the boat lost its transmission-damper plate. I imagine both journeys were difficult trips for both boats.

A SAILING ODYSSEY-Malaysia to the Mediterranean

Upper - Approach to Hurghada Marina
Centre - Maybe a useful dock ... once!
Lower - Outlook changes when you have a woman on-board!

David and Betty had been very generous with their help, to us epitomising the relationships that develop between yacht owners with *problems* and those that can provide *help*. This camaraderie is the best part of travelling in a large group as there is always an expert (from a doctor to a refrigeration mechanic) available for the cost of a couple of bottles of wine, or less!

EL TUR, EGYPT ... 16th MAY 2010
Lat: 28°14'21N, Long: 033°36'47E

From Hurghada we planned to go to the military town of El Tur, Egypt, on the eastern side of the gulf (whereas all our previous stopovers have been on the western shoreline where it is safer to travel). Until this latitude, where the eastern coastline becomes Egypt, the east coastline of the Red Sea is Saudi Arabian territory and described as hostile towards yachties from a military point of view. I did meet a Kiwi sailor who ventured into a Saudi coastal town for rumored 'cheap' fuel and who was promptly arrested by military forces and taken to a town inland from the coast. He was put through a wringer and eventually returned to his yacht just in time to see two soldiers walking off with the outboard motor from his dinghy. With some bravado he wrestled the outboard back from the thieves and returned to his yacht. He got cheap fuel but, was it worth it? *No!*

The crossing to El Tur entailed a night's anchorage at Endeavour Bay which is more mid-Gulf and the following morning crossing the shipping lanes, again, this time from west to east. We were entertained with the sight of a submarine accompanied by a warship, nationality unknown.

We were attracted to crossing to the eastern side of the Red Sea as El Tur is a town located in Egypt, which wraps around the Suez Canal and down to the Gulf of Aqbab. El Tur is a military town - surprise, surprise (it's a well-known fact that the eastern shores of the Red Sea prickle with military) and El Tur has a well-earned reputation for trapping yachts, for days on end, as the winds from the north are channeled through two parallel mountain ranges. These mountains somehow accelerate the winds significantly making the town very windy, dusty and the open ocean seas rough. As a result of the constant strong winds and sheltered harbour, El Tur is a mecca, internationally, for wind surfers and has a hotel on the beach which seems to cater for them exclusively. While we were waiting for weaker winds to arrive the expert wind-surfers provided great entertainment.

We tried to leave El Tur three times and were driven back each time by rough seas. The third attempt was made in convoy with friends first encountered in Aden, Greg and Beverly in **'SV Farjara'** but again we turned back. They carried on, much to their eventual sorrow as they ended up anchoring behind a shallow reef pretty much in the open ocean swell.

With my 1st mate going *'mental'* at being trapped in El Tur for 5 days, at 22:00 on the 21st May, 2010, in calm conditions, I decided to go for a fourth attempt at leaving. We soon caught up with 'SV Farjara', their yacht having suffered a failure in the drive line

Left upper - Beverly sighting submarine.
Upper right - El Tur is a military town ... but, famous worldwide for wind surfing.
Centre - Submarine transiting Suez Canal.
Lower left - Central Business District of El Tur. A poor military town with few public stores.
Lower right - Dust collected on HF radio antenna from atmosphere during stay in El Tur. Thick dust was all over DJV.

assembly between the gearbox and the propeller shaft. We towed them for a short time until a 30 knot NW'er developed and they were able to sail much faster than we could tow them. Without mechanical propulsion, 'SV Farjara' had a *huge* problem getting to Port Suez and a bigger problem getting towed into the Port Suez Yacht Club. In the end they were weeks behind us entering the Mediterranean and we never saw them again.

PORT SUEZ, EGYPT, 24TH MAY 2010
Lat: 29°56'85N, Long: 032°34'36E

The Port Suez Yacht Club is located on the western shore, at the southern-most end of the Suez Canal. It is a poor club and provides few services other than showers/toilets and laundry facilities and a small ill-equipped cafe. I wondered what numbers made up the membership as the facilities were so poorly maintained. On the plus side, it has the most astonishing parade of shipping passing through the Canal, *very* close to its boundary.

TOUR OF CAIRO MUSEUM, THE PYRAMIDS AND SPHINX, 27TH MAY 2010

We decided to do an overnight tour from Port Suez marina to Cairo, travelling by a privately owned and driven car which we had hired. In hindsight, it was the best way to get around Cairo though a coach tour might have been cheaper. The journey from Port Suez marina was around 130 kilometres through barren sandy desert and it was very obvious

Upper - Port Suez Yacht Club.
Centre - DJV happy to be resting at Port Suez.
Lower - 1st Mate Beverly, enjoying the passing parade of ships from the Canal. Can you read the name of the ship in the background?

that if you have no water, you would quickly perish; this was true **Lawrence of Arabia** country.

At one 'drink' stop we were attracted by the sight of a woman leading a donkey with a goat balancing on its back. Our driver, who knew no English somehow made us understand these women were **'Bedouin'** people who came in from the hostile desert to make a few tourist dollars with such performances. Why didn't I patronise them? The thought of wheeling and dealing with a much better bargainer than me, was just too much.

At regular intervals along the way we witnessed army installations and tank armaments. The whole country seems to be on a *war* footing just ready and waiting for someone to 'have-a-go'. I guess this whole region has been on that footing for as long as history books have been written.

CAIRO MUSEUM AND CITY, 17TH MAY 2010

The visit to the Cairo Museum was worthwhile although generally I'm not very interested in visiting such establishments. What made the difference on this occasion were some of Tutankhamen's treasures excavated from his tomb in the Valley of the Kings in Luxor in 1922, by Howard Carter and George Herbert, 5th Earl of Carnarvon. Tutankhamen was just a young boy when he died, but, as was the custom, a vastly expensive and elaborate memorial to his reign was built in his memory. (I've since been advised the tombs are more about a belief in the afterlife and the person needs all that gear to help them on their journey, rather than a memorial to the person.) We had seen Tutankhamen's tomb when we were touring the Valley of the Kings in Luxor and had been told some of the 'goodies' had been taken to Cairo – and here they were. Many other treasures were scattered around the world in many other museums.

Wonderful as it was, Beverly was of the opinion Tutankhamen's treasures were very poorly displayed as the glass cases were not airtight and the museum not air-conditioned. In the middle of this large city the air was far from pure and always polluted by the traffic. I only rated the visit 6 out of 10 because of the poor display, hordes of other tourists and heavily armed Security guards.

TOUR OF PYRAMIDS AND SPHINX, 28TH MAY 2010

The *stars* of the two days were undoubtedly the Pyramids and Sphinx. What wonderful man-made wonders of the world these are. We were taken to a suburb of Cairo adjacent to these antiquities and introduced to the owner of a number of camels and horses. The suggested plan for the tour was for Bev to ride a horse and me a camel. **But,** what was it going to cost? Nobody was prepared to tell us, all they wanted to do was get us on our steads, *fast.* That's when the penny dropped with me – the fee would be stated once you were mounted, from where, three metres above ground level on a cranky, ugly camel (whom I was certain, from the look in his/her eyes, had developed an instant dislike of me) it would be very difficult to reject or negotiate the deal. Therefore, I became what's known in Australia as *'short tempered, bordering on abusive'* and refused to get on the long-legged beast. We insisted the unveiling of the fee was necessary to get our custom. $103.00 for the two of us! I had immediate serious, second thoughts about this journey but Beverly being more generous than me voted for the continuation of the venture.

She was right to insist as the camel and horse tour gave us the best possible viewing angles for both *wonders*. The animals were led by a 15 year old lad whom I felt sorry for, trudging for the 3-4 kilometres, through loose desert sand wearing just flimsy thongs on his feet. The older Guide (about 30 to 40) and mounted very comfortably on a fit looking horse was very attentive to our needs. All was swinging along well until we re-entered the town.

Passing through a narrow back-street alley our caravan came to an abrupt halt and we realised now was the time for our two guides to put the screws on for their *tip*. We had not prepared our plan of attack for this moment and Beverly was too quick to pull E£100 (US$16.00) from her purse, onto which the older Arab swooped viciously, like an eagle from on high.

In the meantime, I had given the kid US$7.00 to which he immediately screwed up his nose shouting *"Not enough, not*

> *Just take my word, the wonders are worth a visit but bear in mind you will be haunted by the unscrupulous Egyptians to part you from your money at every turn.*

Upper left - A trick the guides train you in.
Upper right - Not sure we ever became good friends?
Lower - Beverly and me on our respective mounts.

enough". I was taken aback by his vehemence; I had thought he was such a nice little kid! Not so when it came to tips and his hostility screwed another US$7.00 from me.

In the meantime the older guide was approaching for a tip from me. "Get lost; Bev just paid you our tip." Not bloody likely, that was from Bev and now he wanted E$100.00 from me too! I looked down to the ground from my high perch and wondered how many bones I would break if I did a sliding de-mount of the camel. And on the way down what would the camel do; bolt? There seemed no way out (as is designed by these guys) than to coughed up another E$100.00 and I felt ashamed about the situation I had let myself be led into as I *hate, hate* being duped for any amount, or reason.

To round off the insult on returning to where we started, we were shepherded into a large showroom operated by the camel/horse owner and his wife where staff start hammering you to buy perfumes, clothing, anything. **Not bloody likely.** Away we sped back to Port Suez and the protection of DJV.

Just take my word, the wonders are worth a visit but bear in mind you will be haunted by the unscrupulous Egyptians to part you from your money at every turn. Some tips based on experience:

- Never pay anyone asking for a fee in a 'Free' toilet.
- Never hand over an E£100 note to pay for an E£5 item. You will find there quickly gathers an Egyptian mob which definitely saw you only

hand over an E£10 note and hence you've just lost E£90.
- Never get on a camel or horse, prior to a pyramids tour before knowing what the fee is.
- Be prepared to have the guides of the camel and horse insist on a *large* tip and keep in mind, *no matter what you offer initially,* they will *always* seek to get at least double your offer out of you. Just make sure your first offer is *way-down-low.* Remember, you will be three metres off the ground on the back of an ugly camel, in a back street, when the threatening move is made.
- Begging is a skilled trade and practiced by kids from five years old on the streets.
- You will inevitably get 'stung' as they are very, very experienced ... just start being very conscious of this Egyptian trait.
- We can now see another connection to the phrase "To be gypped", besides it's more usual link to gypsies.

CHAPTER 17

SUEZ CANAL PASSAGE ... 29ᵀᴴ MAY 2010

Shipping of all sizes travel through the Suez Canal in groups which vary in numbers dramatically. At an average width of 200 metres, the canal does not have the width to allow two-way shipping traffic, therefore, convoys of ships travel to and fro in single file and depending on how many ships in a convoy depends on how often the convoys are allowed through in each direction. It seemed to me there was no regular routine to their movements.

The water is subject to strong tidal currents of up to two knots. Speed on the Canal is limited to eight knots for all vessels, no trouble for DJV which has trouble averaging five knots under power.

All ships and yachts take on a dedicated pilot (with the yachts and boats up to 'tug' size, having a lesser qualified pilot on-board). The pilot changes at Ismailia, a town marking the halfway point of the journey of approximately 45 nmiles for each half, with

The cost of the passage was a very reasonable US$245.00 for DJV.

A SAILING ODYSSEY-Malaysia to the Mediterranean

Upper - 'Welcome to Egypt'.
Centre - DJV motoring at five knots ... large ships, at least eight!
Lower - Looks like a 'David and Goliath' battle. A bottle-small fishing boat against a massive ship.

Port Said as the final destination. On entering the marina at Ismailia, yachts can stay as long as they like.

Many yachties organise tours to Luxor, the Aswan Dam and Cairo from here.

The cost of the passage was a very reasonable US$245.00 for DJV. As hard as I tried, I was unable to find out how much the large ships paid to transit the Suez Canal - I suspect it's quite a large sum. When naval/military shipping transits the Canal all other shipping is held at anchor and the government of the naval ship pays double the going rate.

So, off we went. My policy regarding running the motors is to restrict engine speed to a maximum of 3,200 rpm. The first pilot on board whacked the throttle full-forward and had them spinning at 5,000 rpm. *"That won't do at all"* I thought and mentally prepared myself for my first fight with an Arab. I pulled both throttles back to 4,000 rpm and said *"**Maximum**"* loudly and firmly and had no more trouble. It took DJV 10 hours to travel the 45 nmiles - we were the slowest vessel by far.

On approaching Ismailia the waters become choked with green weed. Probably the lack of drainage of these waters but it became a real problem as they heaped up between the hulls of the catamaran and choked the motors. All I could do was slow our speed and lift each motor in turn to clear the weed. The pilot wasn't very happy about this as it extended our time to the mid-point marina ... ***too bad mate!***

A SAILING ODYSSEY-Malaysia to the Mediterranean

Upper - Massive ships mixing with midget sailboats.
Center - Passing under the 'Shohada 25 January Bridge' or the 'Egyptian-Japanese Friendship Bridge'
Lower - Swing bridges to allow quick access across the canal.

We couldn't fail to notice how difficult it would be to take possession of the Canal. Its shorelines on both sides prickle with Egyptian military and they have floating pontoons and swing bridges, ready to swivel across at a moment's notice, so they can be at the *'trouble spot'*, no matter which side, quickly. There's also a very long, high bridge across and at least one tunnel under the canal.

PORT SAID, EGYPT
Lat: 31°17'08N, Long: 032°20'11E

At the far northern end of the canal is Port Said which has a dreadful reputation for corruption. I decided to motor through without stopping but had to drop off our 2nd pilot. The first pilot we had was very corrupt and in our ignorance (when comparing payments with other yachties later), we had given him much more money than we should have. The pilot on the second leg was quite the opposite. But, be prepared to grease-the-palms of the crew picking up the pilot from your vessel in Port Said harbour ... although in the confusion involved in transiting the harbour at 22:00, I was able to out-fumble them on this occasion. The fact DJV had just picked up a ten metre length of strapping around one of her propellers at exactly that time and was travelling in tight circles while Beverly raised the motor and cut away the strap may have been a helpful diversion.

On approaching the drop-off point for our pilot I became very aware of four ferries crossing the harbour (which is only 250 metres wide) two from the right hand shore and two from the left. They have this incredible system of releasing these ferries from each shore simultaneously and have them converge in the middle of the harbour in a scissor action. Not knowing what they were up to initially created a mental concussion in this lad's brain until I got the hang of it.

On clearing the Heads of Port Said harbour, my 1st mate somehow found the energy to perform a Go-Go dance to celebrate being clear of Egypt and the Red Sea. We were in seventh heaven! *Cyprus and the Mediterranean, here we come!*

CHAPTER 18

PAPHOS, CYPRUS ... FROM 2nd JUNE, 2010
Lat: 34° 45' 26N ... Long: 032° 24' 48E

Our original plans on leaving Port Said, Egypt, had been to turn right and sail across to Israel. We had booked into a marina and all was set until a week before our exiting Port Said, the Israeli Military boarded a ship heading for the Gaza Strip and killed several would-be terrorists. That put an end to yachts travelling to and fro from Egypt to Israel, at least for a short time.

Our next best choice was Cyprus which would be a long sail of 211 nmiles and another two days at sea before we reached civilization again. (Civilisation as we remembered it, that is, which **did not** include any of the Asian landings since leaving Malaysia.) In having made that **outrageous** statement about Asia, I'm challenged to explain a bit about the boundaries of Asia. Surely in travelling 6200nmiles we had often been outside the boundaries of Asia? Not really! The **western boundary** of Asia includes Yemen and Saudi Arabia (but, not the countries on the western shoreline of the Red Sea). The **northern boundary** is Eastern Turkey (but, not the Black Sea), Georgia, Armenia,

Azerbaijan and nearly all of Russia. The ***eastern boundary*** comprises Japan and both North and South Koreas, Taiwan and the Philippines. While the ***southern boundary*** includes Papua New Guinea, Indonesia, Sri Lanka, India, Pakistan, Oman and back to Yemen. And it includes ***all*** the countries surrounded by these boundaries. Boring stuff really but important to some! (If you're interested Google 'Asian Boundaries' for further discussions.)

There are three shipping channels entering/leaving Port Said *(which in fact has two ports)* and in the blackness of night the scramble of red/green/yellow and white lights was hard to read. But once again, the chart plotter came to the rescue and made the exit possible without incident. Winds were ESE to start and perfect for the destination we had in mind but they didn't last and we were back into the routine of motor/sail/motor. Generally speaking it was a good crossing taking 48 hours to cover the 211 nmiles ... an average speed of 4.4 knots.

We entered the almost pitch black Paphos Harbour on the south west corner of Cyprus, at 22:00, and found it to be very small and packed with fishing/charter/power/sailing boats of all shapes and sizes. It was a nightmare and we were expected to sort out an anchorage in only the soft glow of street lighting around the harbour walls. In the end I snuggled DJV against a larger catamaran tied stern-to a pontoon and nobody yelled and screamed. The owners of the cat were not living aboard.

The Greek water police were stern, even at 22:00 and Bev and I had to power up to the wharf on the

Upper - Paphos harbour ... small and packed.
Centre - Amphitheatre lower south coast of Cyprus.
Lower - One of many ancient ruins ... near Paphos harbour.

dinghy, find the police office and jump through the usual customs/immigration and harbour-master hoops, on this occasion involving pulling the customs officer out of bed. All worked out in the end and we all seemed to part friends.

Beverly and I felt like *two-bobs-worth-of-chewed-string* from the long journey and I guess that was to be expected, as we still hadn't truly 'landed'. In fact the feeling of mental and physical stress stayed with me for 3-4 months with the unconscious pressure of months of preparation and then the five months journey over 6,200 nmiles *(11,500 kilometres)* proving a greater stress than I had imagined.

Paphos is a mecca for British tourists. They swarm here by the thousands and many are conned into using mortgages to buy apartments *on-the-tick,* which they can't afford. The sales pitch is *"Your in-comings from rentals will pay your monthlies".* Well, it's often proven that they won't as so many of these apartments come back onto the market. But a good place to buy property if you have cash.

Cyprus is a huge rocky island with a small section of the northern area now occupied by Turkey. Turkey invaded Cyprus in 1972 and there is still and always will be (according to the Greek women I spoke to in the Tourist Bureau office) great friction between the two countries. A visit to the capital, Nicosia, reveals the city itself has been segregated and you have to pass through an immigration post to obtain a visa to visit the Turkish half of the city.

Cyprus has an impressive history as one would expect in this part of the world and there are many archaeological treasures to visit. And the island is surrounded by crystal clear water, for which the Mediterranean is justly famous. Given these assets, we enjoyed an overdue rest here and left on the 12th May, 2010, for Lara Bay, a small bay 12 nmiles north of Paphos. Then it was a 77 nmiles motor/sail across to Fineke, Turkey accompanied by *'SV Kleiner Bar'* who had arrived in Paphos a few days after us.

CHAPTER 19

FINEKE, TURKEY ... FROM 14TH JUNE, 2010
Lat: 36° 17' 60N, Long: 030° 08' 91E

We hadn't booked into the marina at Fineke and therefore anchored in the adjacent shallows in company with 'SV Kleiner Bar'. The next day we transferred to the marina and started a good seven days of R&R. Beverly's departure for Canada was very much on our minds and one morning it seemed appropriate to make a short speech:

Lloyd ... "Beverly, I want you to accept a gift from me as a memento of our time together and of the journey we have successfully completed."

Bev ... "Lloyd, you don't have to do that, it has been an experience I'll always treasure."

Lloyd ... "Well, I thank you for that, but this gift is something special and I have to tell you it cost AU$2700.00."

Bev ... "Lloyd, what have you done?"

Lloyd ... "I've decided to give you the new screecher and want you to help me fit it today".

I was prepared to run and duck for cover but the Canadian took it all in her stride and we had great fun fitting the new sail. (Bev had been urging me to fit this sail - something like a large Genoa or a

A SAILING ODYSSEY-Malaysia to the Mediterranean

Upper - Beverly at a Turkish market.
Centre - Fineke, Turkey with marina in the foreground.
Lower left - Bev cooking up her recent purchases.
Lower right - A tomb on the hillside at Kekova-Simena, Turkey.

very, very big jib - right from the time of its arrival in Langkawi, Malaysia, from New Zealand, where it had been made. She had spotted it early on in her stay on DJV; she could hardly miss it as the only place I had room to store it was for'ard in the cockpit area. At every opportunity, she would bug me by stressing "we must fit the new screecher" or words to that effect. "No Beverley, not until the old sail shreds itself; it will get us to the Mediterranean, just you wait and see." And it did!

Beverly hacked a corner from the old sail and I wrote a message on it as a memento for her of our time together during this great journey:

To Bev ...
A memento of an epic journey from Malaysia to Turkey via the Red Sea...
January to June 2010. A total of 6,200 nmiles
Thank you for your great help and support
Love from Lloyd,
Skipper, Déjà vu III

At Fineke marina we caught up with a few yachts that had journeyed the same route and it was great to swap yarns of the different adventures we had experienced. Fineke is a small town which caters to the visiting yachts very well. It's also an official entry/exit point for yachts arriving/departing Turkey from/to overseas. We relaxed, cleaned Arabian dust from DJV, ate at restaurants, visited open markets which Turkey is famous for, connected to the internet via Vodafone, swam, did a rough inventory of stores not consumed (just to see what had to be eaten in the near future) **and Beverly began preparations for leaving DJV.**

After our leisurely week we took off again to see more of Turkey in the company of 'SV Kleiner Bar'. We sailed to a wonderful protected bay near the island of Kaleköy at Kekova-Simena topped by an ancient castle of the **Knights of Rhodes.**

When in Turkish waters, it is very easy to inadvertently stray into Greece given how the islands are distributed between the two countries. On our quest to see more of Turkey, we accidently visited the Greek island of Meyisti which is just 1.1 nmiles from the closest shoreline of Turkey and 3.1 nmiles SW of the Turkish town of Kas. It looked like a good anchorage and only as we got nearer did I realise my error. *"Beverly, all the flags onshore are blue and white, I think we've stumbled onto Greek territory, quick, down with the Turkish flag."*

"What have you done *Ol' Man*"? Bev knew how to hit-the-nerve.

It was a gorgeous little area and although we weren't game to go ashore *(we had no visa)* I was surprised some Greek authority didn't pull alongside to ask us what-the-hell we were doing here?

BEVERLY'S DEPARTURE FROM DJV ... 28TH JUNE, 2010

28th June 2010 came all too soon, a very sad day for Bev and me as she was leaving DJV. After six months together we had developed a close and strong relationship. You can't beat experience and 1st mate Beverly was able to exhibit her skills learned from previously racing mono

Upper - Beverly and Lloyd with DJV backdrop.
Lower left - Memento of trip from Skipper to 1st mate.
Lower right - Beverly leaving Kas, Turkey. A tearful soul ... happy but unhappy!

A SAILING ODYSSEY—Malaysia to the Mediterranean

yachts and at the same time learnt lots about multi-hull sailing ... it is different! With our strong personalities we had our moments of stress and debate, but always worked through them to find our relationship as strong as ever. Beverly never hesitated to stress her opinion and a compromise was often reached to both our satisfactions. We had a contract which had her agreeing to pay her share of expenses and never did she arrive late with a due payment. Most importantly she was great in the galley although **harsh** with outdated tins and much old food went overboard in a flash. I'm sure I would have survived eating any of it. Bev was an adventurer and never hesitated the call to be hauled up the mast when required. Here was a woman with ideals of immaculate cleanliness *(driving me mad at times)* and to her sorrow, something I was not great at emulating.

And all of a sudden in a flood of tears, she was gone ...

For me, with Beverly gone, the journey from Malaysia to the Mediterranean had finally ended and I could now safely claim to have successfully guided DJV and her crew through the many challenges of this voyage. It took almost exactly five months and during that time Déjà vu covered 6,158 nmiles.

I have been asked many times, "would I do the same journey again"?

On reflection, I feel once in a lifetime is enough, partly because of the personal risks now involved in the Arabian

Sea and Gulf of Aden. I'm certain in my heart we were lucky during many of the rough times we went through, the most worrying being -

- *Coming out of Aceh, Indonesia when the 'tidal wave' swept under us.*

- *The rough two and a half days weather east of Sri Lanka when DJV and crew were subjected to such a tough time.*

- *During the same time/area, at night when the autopilot decided to stop working.*

- *South of Cochin, India, at night, when we came within centimeters of running down a fishing boat.*

- *And later, during the same night, just a few nmiles south of Cochin when a large power boat was intent on ramming us.*

- *The message received from friends off Oman, 'freighters were running at night without a single light showing' to avoid detection by pirate, was scary.*

- *My naivety across the Gulf of Aden that pirates weren't a threat to us ... which the US Coalition Warship awoke me to.*

- *Having DJV swung around as though on a merry-go-round by a whirlpool, when entering the Red Sea, in the dark ... an adrenaline pumping thrill.*

- *Having the Eritrean Navy come alongside wanting to check our papers with a soldier brandishing an AK-47 machine gun.*

- *Then another bunch of Sudanese soldiers powering out from a Fort to try to force us into their Bay.*

- *Egypt is a place I will avoid with fervor ... just take good care of your money if you decide to visit!*

Otherwise it was a 'Cake-walk'.

On the other hand, maybe I would do it again if certain conditions applied, primarily that there would be more crew to share the watch-work. Sharing a 24/7 period for weeks between only two people means both soon suffer from mental and physical strain. Whether you strike up a 2, 4 or 6 hour watch period the pressure of a rough ride and frequent interruptions to sleep soon build into unshakable fatigue. With three or four crew the journey would be so much easier as the rest periods would be longer.

But a larger crew would mean housing and feeding more people and the need for a larger ship. (It would have been impossible to have squeezed even one more person onto DJV.) And so begins a spiral into another realm of cost and investment. Outside my league I'm sure and that's why I'm happy with my 10 metre Seawind 1000 ... happy to have done what I have done and not to attempt it again.

In any case, for me, the question is also *hypothetical* because of current politics; the moment the Somalia pirates squeezed the triggers of their guns and killed the four Americans on 'SV Quest' in the Arabian Sea through 2011 ... was the moment the game was over for ordinary, unprotected sailors taking this route to the Mediterranean. And this will likely be the case for years/decades to come. How will this situation ever be turned around?

Those sailors still wanting to get their ship from Malaysia to the Mediterranean are paying *huge* money to have it shipped and then more money to fly themselves to Turkey to meet their vessel. I was lucky on a number of counts to have sailed through when I did in 2010 ... as I'm confident DJV was one of the last privately owned sailing vessels to do so!

Now I have the Med to learn about and I know it's going to be a hard but exciting playground; but maybe it will lead to another book. I can already see I won't be short of material!

GLOSSARY ... As I see it!

Abeam ... 90° to the ship's centreline.

Aft ... The back end of a yacht ... (blunt end).

Anti-fouling ... A paint mixture applied to the hulls, usually from the waterline down to reduce the growth of barnacles and other ocean nasties. With this growth comes a reduction in boat speed. Antifoul is usually applied every two years.

Attacking angle ... Is the angle of the wind across the deck. (See 'Reach').

Auto Pilot ... Comprises two units; the brain which is embedded in the chart plotter and the drive assembly, in DJV's case, bolted to one of the steering wheels.

Beat ... Closely related to 'tacking' as to 'beat' is to sail as close as possible in the direction the wind is coming.

Bommies ...	Coral growths which can grow to enormous size and become a common navigation hazard, usually in shallow bays. They are very unforgiving if you run into one at great speed. It can be the end-of-your-yacht!
Boom ...	The aluminium (can be wood or other material) spar that runs horizontally along the base of the mainsail to hold out the foot/bottom, of the sail.
Bow ...	The leading edge (pointy end) of the yacht.
Broaching ...	When a sailing vessel is forced into a sudden sharp turn, often heeling heavily and in smaller vessels sometimes leading to capsize. Usually occurs when **too much sail** is set for a strong gust of wind and the vessel becomes over-powered. Mono yachts are more susceptible to broaching whereas a multihull is more likely to bury its bows, also possibly leading to a dangerous loss of control and capsize!
Cake-walk ...	Australian slang meaning 'it couldn't be easier'!

Chart-plotter ...   A chart plotter is a device providing an electronic version of printed navigation charts as used by many sailors even now and all that was available until recent decades. Chart plotters give your exact location on the screen from connecting to 10-12 overhead satellites. I wouldn't leave the harbour without one.

Clew ...   Lower aft (back) corner of a fore-and-aft sail. (See fore-and-aft sail).

Cockpit ...   Where you stand to steer the boat. A catamaran cockpit is very different from that on a mono-hull vessel, primarily due to the wider beam of a cat. DJV has a beam of 5.91 metres whereas a mono of the same length would be closer to 3.00 metres. The cockpit is centrally located on the cat and is much like a living room. The Seawind 1000 has almost 360° visibility and in a cloud-burst you can stay dry!

Collision formula ...   A quick method to determine if you're on a collision course with another ship. Staying stationary yourself on-board, align a vertical fixture on your ship with the other approaching ship. If the other ship appears to be moving to the left of the vertical alignment it will pass across your bow. If it moves to the right, it will pass astern of you. If it stays in the same alignment, you *will* collide!

Currency ... In the book, I often quote an item I've purchased in the currency of the country I'm buying it in (e.g. Ringgits in Malaysia, Baht in Thailand etc.) and then give a conversion to the Australian Dollar in the hopes that people reading this conversion will gain a more accurate idea of the value of the item. ***Otherwise, who other than a Malaysian would know what 100 Ringgits is worth?*** One other thing, I never have enough currency!

Déjà vu III Website ... Feel free to checkout my Website at: www.svdejavu.com

Drogue ... My drogue is a very small, strong, parachute (approximately half metre in diameter) which is dragged behind your yacht when it is going too fast. It can also be used to steer by altering

	the bridle lengths attaching the drogue to the vessel if you have lost your rudder. A drogue can also be made from anything that will create drag-through-the-water (tyres, crates, and miles of rope/line). My drogue is ineffectual under 10 knots of boat speed.
Fetch ...	The distance across the water from a solid object, e.g. when we crossed the Indian Ocean, the 'fetch' was from the shores of NE India in the Bay of Bengal, to DJV – a distance of about 1,000 nmiles. This gave the wave action a long distance in which to build up and (taking into account that wave action is also directly related to wind speed) given the winds there of 35 knots, waves were big and fast moving. In contrast, if the fetch is 300 metres the wave action has no time to build, whatever the wind speed.
Foot ...	The lower/bottom edge of a sail.
For'ard ...	Towards the bow (the pointy end) of the vessel.

Fore-and-aft sail rigging ...	Most modern yachts have a sail layout which is 'fore-and-aft' rigged, i.e. the sails are laid along the line of the keel, or, along the centreline of the hull/s.
Foredeck ...	The area for'ard of the cockpit where on a multihull, you would find the trampolines.
Fuel definitions ...	Déjà vu has two 9.9 hp petrol powered outboards and the fuel they run on is petrol. In Australia we sometimes call petrol 'petroleum'. In Asia and most countries around the Mediterranean it's called benzene. Most yachts have engines that run on dieseline, as it's called in Australia. Most other places I've visited around the world, call it diesel.
Gybe or Jibe ...	When it's necessary to turn the **stern** across the wind to change direction of travel. It is best if the crew has a firm control of a gybe as serious injury and even death can be the end result of being hit with a swinging boom. And serious gear damage can ensue. *(See Preventer).*

Halyard ... A rope (can be a braided wire) used for raising/lowering sails up/down the mast. They are usually the strongest rope available such as a brand called 'Spectra'.

Heave-to ... When sailing, *'heaving-to'* is the action that allows a skipper to turn his vessel across the wind to create a 'stalling' effect. This can be to allow crew to rest, even in rough conditions, or to undertake essential repairs. Heaving-to requires the mainsail to be locked hard to one side so the wind will spill from it readily and the rudder held on the opposite lock; all things being equal the vessel will almost stall completely (there will be a minor drift factor if it's done correctly and every vessel will react differently). Some sailors also leave the jib in place, only backfilled. ***This manoeuvre must be practiced.***

The alternative to heaving-to is to deploy a Para-anchor and hold the bow directly into the wind ... but heaving-to is much simpler and quicker to employ.

Then there are the sailors who will deploy the Para-anchor in unison with the heaving-to action.

This writer had an experience recently while sailing solo from Croatia to Italy, when the auto-pilot failed. I was scratching my head for a while as I needed both hands to fit the replacement, who was going to steer? **Hark** ... why not 'heave-to'? It worked a treat and with a new auto-pilot in place, we were under way again within the hour.

Radios ...

DJV has two radios. One is VHF (very high frequency) which strangely enough usually only has an effective range of around 30-40 nmiles. In the Arabian Sea, however, I found we were picking up VHF signals from around 100 nmiles away. I think this was because the signal was being transmitted across a flat ocean from a warship using an antenna which was mounted high above the waterline.

Our other radio is HF (high frequency) and this unit can bounce signals from the ionosphere and back to earth for thousands of miles, depending on which frequency you are using. This is the radio we use in conjunction with the 'Sailmail' email system *(not to be confused with the Yahoo Internet system)*. I'm not at all an expert in such radios so there will undoubtedly be radio buffs who will snigger at my description.

Insurance at sea ...

Owners of sailing/power vessels have the option of insuring their vessel against mishaps whilst at sea (much the same as most insure their motor vehicles on land). *But,* unlike motor insurance, it is not usually mandatory. If an owner wants to take the risk themselves, they may. Only sailing in the Mediterranean does it appear to be mandatory, with most countries wanting to see the insurance papers for your vessel at the time of clearing into their country and then this request is always followed up when entering a marina. I had DJV insured whilst in Australian waters, but, on leaving to sail through to Asia I let it lapse due

Joe Ziudzinski ...   to the high cost. DJV is insured in the Mediterranean.

Joe Ziudzinski ...   A sailor/owner of a Seawind 1000 who has written a great Website about his and his wife Kathy's adventures off the east coast of Australia, New Zealand and the South Pacific Islands and Alaska above Canada. Website: www.katiekat.net

Log ...   A book in which the captain will make a regular note (six hourly in my case) on conditions and happenings on and around the vessel, e.g. weather, distance travelled etc. ... death of a crew person!

Luff ...   The for'ard edge of a for-and-aft sail. With the mainsail the edge that runs up the mast is the 'luff'.

Nautical mile ...   One kilometre = 1000 metres

One mile = 1609 metres

One nautical mile = 1852 metres

On-the-nose ...   When the wind is coming from exactly the direction your destination lies.

Para anchor ...	In a nutshell ... a Para-anchor (sea anchor) is a life saving device designed along the lines of an aircraft parachute ... only it is deployed from the bow of a vessel in severe weather conditions, or, when the crew are exhausted from fatigue and must have rest. The Para-anchor will hold the bow of a vessel into the wind and allow a liveable life for those on-board until the storm is over. See www.paraanchors.com.au for full details.
Piece-of-cake ...	Same as 'Cake-walk'. (Meaning 'It couldn't be easier')!
Port tack ...	When the wind is crossing the yacht from the port starboard side.
Preventer ...	On DJV, this is a block and tackle arrangement anchored to the aft cleat on each hull and when attached to the boom will *'prevent'* the accidental/unplanned jibing of the boom and mainsail. (See jibing). The preventer ***should always*** be in place when the wind is from directly astern. An unplanned jibe can lead to serious injury and even death and at the least, severe equipment damage.

Reach ...	Explanation of 'Points of sailing' into/away from the wind.
No sailing possible:	DJV will not sail into/across the wind unless the wind is at least $40°$ off the centreline of the vessel, on port or starboard tack.
Close hauled:	When you are sailing from $40°$ to $50°$ off the wind.
Close Reach:	When you're sailing from $50°$ to $70°$ off the wind.
Beam Reach:	When you are sailing from $70°$ to $110°$ off the wind. DJV loves this angle to the wind and will find her best speed, usually 7/8 knots in 15-20 knots of wind.
Broad Reach:	When you're sailing from $110°$ to $140°$ off the wind.
Running:	When the wind is coming from astern - $140°$ to $180°$.
Reef ...	Most of the power when undersail develops from the mainsail. If the wind increases the vessel can quickly become **'over-powered'** and this can lead to excessive speed, which can lead to broaching, or the submarining of the bow/s. Putting a **reef** in the sail by folding some of the sail down/away, reduces the

expanse of the sail and hence the power generated by the wind blowing across it.

Registered Ship ... Should you have the ambition of cruising internationally, it will be mandatory for your vessel to be registered as a ship of your own country. The most onerous aspect of this process is to prove ownership. *Overseas it is accepted if a ship is registered, that 'proof-of-ownership' is certain.* **DO NOT** attempt to sail internationally without being in possession of a 'Certificate of Registration'. You won't get far! And in my own case, the people in Canberra were very reasonable to deal with ... although the process is expensive at AU$800+

Rhumb line ... A straight line drawn by the navigator from the present position of the yacht to your destination.

Sailmail ... The SailMail Association is a non-profit association of yacht owners that operates and maintains an email communications system for use by its members. (Taken from the Sailmail 'Home' page). Contact

	www.sailmail.com for all the information.
Sheets ...	Lines/ropes used and attached to various sails to control them.
Snail trail ...	A 'snail trail' is an electronic line drawn on the screen (from behind the image of your vessel) of a chart-plotter leaving visual proof of the route you have taken on that journey.
Starboard tack ...	When the wind is crossing the yacht from the starboard side.
Tack ...	To turn your vessel (to tack) to allow the attacking angle *(see attacking angle)* of the wind to change from port to starboard, or, vice versa. *(Also see 'Gybe').* There's no difference between a gybe and a jibe. Both words mean the same thing.
Trampoline ...	Because of the wide beam on a catamaran there's a huge gap formed between the for'ard third of the two hulls. This is filled with a strong mesh material capable of supporting the weight of several people and most often used for setting the anchor and tending for'ard sails.

Washboards ...   Solid fiberglass/wood/glass/plastic boards that, when in place, will prevent the entry of water, or people (if padlocked), or almost anything from entering the hulls.

Way points ...   Waypoints are produced by the operator of a chart-plotter to mark a destination to which the auto-pilot will steer. A series of waypoints will create a *route* to follow. Waypoints can also be markings on a paper chart.

Route taken from Darwin, Australia through Indonesia, Singapore, Malaysia and Thailand ... from July 2007 through January 2010

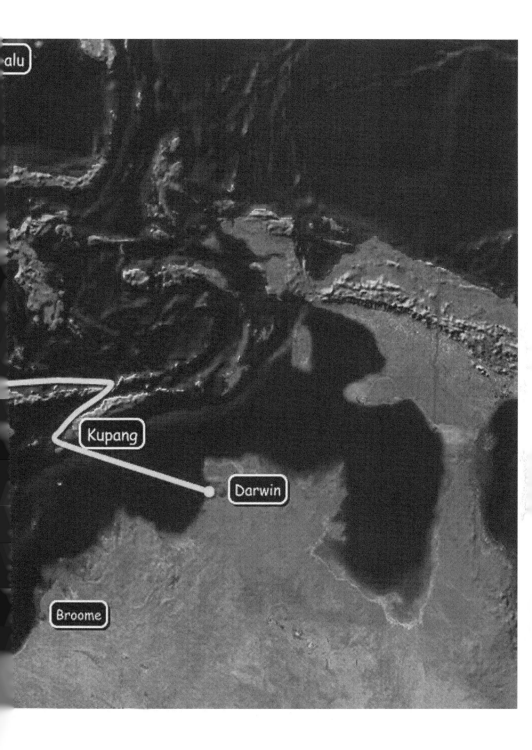

Yellow route ... sailed through 2005
Red route ... sailed through 2006
Green route ... sailed through 2007

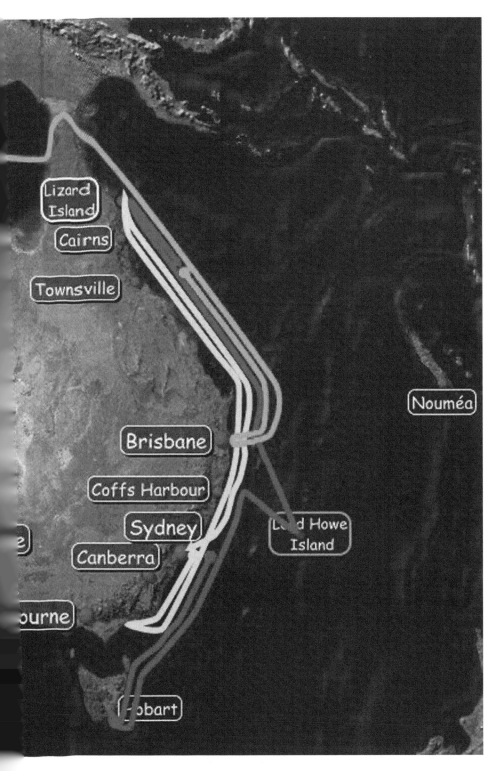

Printed in Great Britain
by Amazon.co.uk, Ltd.,
Marston Gate.